LOOK!

The finished work of Jesus

Mick Mooney

Contents

Foreword 5

Introduction..7

1   The true identity of Jesus 13

2   The finished work of Jesus 17

3   The confused disciples..23

4   No condemnation 27

5   The self-focused disciples......................................29

6   The new creation 33

7   The old and the new 37

8   It's good news! 43

9   The 'Jesus answer' regarding God's work 47

10   The wrong focus...51

11   The modern day 'greatness debate'.......................55

12   The reed and the Rock...59

13   The disciple who loved Jesus 63

14   The disciple whom Jesus loved 67

15	It's not about me!	71
16	Faith, Spirit, Grace and Power	75
17	Fix your eyes on Jesus	81
18	Who is Jesus to you?	85
19	The true Light of the world	89
20	You need to see the reality	93
21	Don't try to pay twice	97
22	The transformation process	101
23	Heavenly results	105
24	Your understanding Father	109
25	The bride	113
26	Our salvation	117
27	The church	121
28	The preacher	127
29	The Corinthians	131
30	The Galatians	135

Conclusion: You are radically loved 139

Acknowledgments 143

About the author 147

For my Mum,

Thanks for always encouraging me to chase after my dreams.

Foreword

Many books have been written about Jesus Christ that inspire us to want to know him more intimately. While that's an admirable goal for an author, the book you are about to read does something greater. **Look! The Finished Work of Jesus** doesn't just cause the reader to hunger to know him more; it fills that very hunger by presenting Jesus in such a way that you actually sense his loving embrace as you read the book.

As I read this book, I found myself delighting again and again in some of the things Mick Mooney has written here. While this book will certainly teach you, it does more than that; it will touch you with a personal awareness of divine agape being expressed to you even as you read. More than once I felt as if my Father's arms were holding me close while his voice whispered of his love to me through these chapters.

Religion complicates and confuses people by its demands and harsh scrutiny of our behaviour. The grace of God stands in stark contrast to religion by assuring us that because of the finished work of Jesus, we are not only in good standing with God but are actually cherished by him. Grace frees us from trying to prove anything to him, to others or even to ourselves. Mick has a firm grasp on that reality and writes in a way that causes others to understand it too.

The religious climate of the world today promotes the idea that we need to do certain things to earn God's blessings and to make spiritual progress. This is a book that is counter-cultural to the world of legalism. It points us to Jesus Christ and causes us to see and really believe that what he has done on our behalf is indeed sufficient and that there is nothing left for us to do other than live out of the reality of his finished work.

I predict that **Look! The Finished Work of Jesus** is going to be used by our Father to set many people free from the prison of religious performance and usher them into the rest that only comes by living in his grace.

Steve McVey
Author, Grace Walk

Introduction

Every Christian has an individual testimony, a past that is truly unique. Our lives may indeed be different, but they are all knit together with a common thread. That thread is the person of Jesus Christ.

Jesus has opened our eyes to a whole new reality; a heavenly reality. He has showed us a whole new way of understanding God and the relationship we have with him.

In the world today, no-one's true identity is more hotly debated than that of Jesus Christ's. When he walked the earth 2,000 years ago the debate began and it has not ceased since, indeed it has only intensified.

The list of opinions on his true identity found throughout the Bible continues to mirror current opinions today. A small sample of some popular opinions includes:

- ◈ A mad man[1]
- ◈ A good man[2]
- ◈ A prophet[3]
- ◈ A false prophet[4]
- ◈ A miracle worker[5]
- ◈ A con man[6]
- ◈ A heretic[7]
- ◈ A drunk[8]
- ◈ A glutton[8]
- ◈ A wizard[9]
- ◈ A mere man[10]
- ◈ A myth that never existed[11]

---

[1] Many of them said, 'He is demon-possessed and raving mad. Why listen to him?' *John 10:20*

[2] Among the crowds there was widespread whispering about him. Some said, 'He is a good man.' *John 7:12*

[3] When Jesus entered Jerusalem, the whole city was stirred and asked, 'Who is this?' The crowds answered, 'This is Jesus, the prophet from Nazareth in Galilee.' *Matthew 21:10-11*

[4] 'Does our law condemn anyone without first hearing him to find out what he is doing?' They replied, 'Are you from Galilee, too? Look into it, and you will find that a prophet does not come out of Galilee.' *John 7:52*

[5] 'Where did this man get these things?' they asked. 'What's this wisdom that has been given him, that he even does miracles! Isn't this the carpenter? Isn't this Mary's son and the brother of James, Joseph, Judas and Simon? Aren't his sisters here with us?' And they took offense at him. *Mark 6:3*

[6] Others replied, 'No, he deceives the people.' But no one would say anything publicly about him for fear of the Jews. *John 7:12-13*

[7] Then the high priest tore his clothes and said, 'He has spoken blasphemy! Why do we need any more witnesses? Look, now you have heard the blasphemy.' *Matthew 26:65*

[8] The Son of Man came eating and drinking, and they say, 'Here is a glutton and a drunkard, a friend of tax collectors and 'sinners'. But wisdom is proved right by her actions. *Matthew 11:19*

[9] But when the Pharisees heard this, they said, 'It is only by Beelzebub, the prince of demons, that this fellow drives out demons'. *Matthew 12:24*

[10] 'We are not stoning you for any of these,' replied the Jews, 'but for blasphemy, because you, a mere man, claim to be God.' *John 10:33*

[11] We did not follow cleverly invented stories when we told you about the power and coming of our Lord Jesus Christ, but we were eyewitnesses of his majesty. *2 Peter 1:16*

Why does God allow mankind to believe such wild and totally inaccurate opinions regarding his Son? He does so because God is not a suppressor of opinions; he is a believer in freedom. It is in his nature to allow mankind the freedom to think and act apart from his leading if we so desire. Indeed, God is never going to force anyone to accept the truth regarding the identity and nature of Jesus. However, he does rejoice whenever an individual gives him permission to reveal this truth to them. It's a revelation that he is pleased to give to anyone who opens their heart to receive it.[12]

> Religion will always try to sell you the lie that God wants to relate to you based on your 'works', but the gospel proclaims the truth that God actually desires to relate with you based on the *finished work* of his Son

God does not create people with a cookie cutter. Like all great artists, he enjoys making each of his creations unique. He has created us all as individuals; indeed, all of us could write our own life story with confidence that it would be unlike anyone else's. However, within our own unique biography, God still wants us to share one common chapter. It's the chapter where we give him permission to reveal the true nature and identity of Jesus to our hearts.

Understanding the true identity and nature of Jesus does not take place in a single moment; it is an ongoing journey. God is not satisfied until we are truly free. It is the promise of freedom that Christ desires to fulfil in the life of every believer. That freedom is not only from sin, but also from the weight of religious obligations and expectations. In many cases the greatest challenge a Christian

---

[12] Simon Peter answered, 'You are the Christ, the Son of the living God.' Jesus replied, 'Blessed are you, Simon son of Jonah, for this was not revealed to you by man, but by my Father in heaven.' *Matthew 16:16-17*

faces is not in letting go of sinful activity; it is in letting go of false religious mindsets.[13]

Our new covenant with God is not based on religious traditions and obligations; it is based on *faith* in the finished work of Jesus. It is this faith that allows us to accept that we are saved by grace, born-again into grace and forever found in grace. God's grace is not simply a point of salvation in our past, it is the very place where we now live!

> *Therefore, since we have been justified through faith, we have peace with God through our Lord Jesus Christ, through whom* **we have gained access by faith into this grace in which we now stand.** *And we rejoice in the hope of the glory of God*
>
> **Romans 5:1-2**

Religion will always try to sell you the lie that God wants to relate to you based on your 'works', but the gospel proclaims the truth that God actually desires to relate with you based on the *finished work* of his Son.

The life of Jesus completely interrupted mankind's obsession with religious obligations, rituals and sacrifices. He put an end to the idea that we could reach God by our own efforts and good works. He revealed a better way—*his way*. It is the new and living way, and it is glorious![14]

Sometimes, even as Christians, we can still cling to our old religious mindsets that demand that we work for our provision, prove

---

[13] See to it that no one takes you captive through hollow and deceptive philosophy, which depends on human tradition and the basic principles of this world rather than on Christ. *Colossians 2:8*

[14] Therefore, brothers, since we have confidence to enter the Most Holy Place by the blood of Jesus, by a new and living way opened for us through the curtain, that is, his body, and since we have a great priest over the house of God, let us draw near to God with a sincere heart in full assurance of faith, having our hearts sprinkled to cleanse us from a guilty conscience and having our bodies washed with pure water. *Hebrews 10:19-22*

ourselves worthy and earn our place in God's presence. We may not say these things out loud, but they remain in our sub-conscious and cause our faith journey to be heavy and burdensome. However, God, in his goodness, is always offering to take that burden off of our shoulders and replace it with the truth of our new covenant reality—*the way has already been prepared for us.*

The reality is that Jesus died not only for the forgiveness of our sins; he also died to establish a brand new covenant in which we could live. In this covenant there is not only forgiveness of sins, but also new life. It is a heavenly agreement, not based on mankind's faithfulness, but on the perfect faithfulness of Jesus. It is eternally guaranteed, not based on mankind's offerings, but on the perfect offering of Jesus. It is a personal relationship in which can God reveal himself as he truly is: the God of all grace.[15]

Most of us, as followers of Jesus, understand the theory that we are loved, but it's often possible to feel a much more tangible sense that we are somehow a disappointment to God or a chronic underachiever in spiritual disciplines. God's heart is to bring us out of this *religious mindset* into the glorious freedom of his grace. The truth is we are radically loved.

This book is written for you, the disciple whom Jesus loves. It is a simple message; it is the gospel message. It is about the good news of God's grace that was established not by your efforts, but by the finished work of the cross.

I pray this book will help you to see the depths of Christ's love for you, and in doing so, that you may rejoice freely in the goodness of God's abundant grace.

---

[15]   And the God of all grace, who called you to his eternal glory in Christ, after you have suffered a little while, will himself restore you and make you strong, firm and steadfast. *1 Peter 5:10*

1 The true identity of Jesus

For Jesus received honour and glory from God the Father when the voice came to him from the Majestic Glory, saying, 'This is my Son, whom I love; with him I am well pleased.'

2 Peter 1:17

Many people in the world today reject the claim that Jesus was a real historical figure. Others accept that he was a real man who walked the earth but still think negatively of him. There are also many people who have a positive opinion concerning his identity, believing that he was a teacher, a religious leader or even a prophet. However, what if he is far greater than all of these personas? What if the reality regarding his true identity is so much greater? What if it is so great that it almost blows our minds? What happens when we allow ourselves to see Jesus from a heavenly point of view?[16]

What if he is bigger than a man, a teacher or a prophet? What if he is bigger than our world, our solar system and our universe? What if he was not merely a man once contained to a human body

---

16   So from now on we regard no one from a worldly point of view. Though we once regarded Christ in this way, we do so no longer. *2 Corinthians 5:16*

but is eternally someone so much more? What if he is the one who contains all things, including the universe? What kind of impact does this have on us? What if his true nature and identity is so radical that it leaves us speechless?[17]

The truth is radical: Jesus is the almighty creator of the universe. He is the source through which everything was created, the power that holds everything together and the reason everything was made in the first place. He is the Son of God.[18]

> What if Jesus is bigger
> than a man,
> a teacher or a prophet?
> What if he is bigger
> than our world,
> our solar system
> and our universe?

He is the one who for all of eternity has literally been holding the entire universe together. It is as if with his right hand he holds one end of the universe, and with his left hand he holds the other end—and in between is over 100 billion light years in space!

Light travels at 300,000 km per second; that roughly equates to a light year being over 9.4 trillion kilometres long. In an attempt to grasp how big the universe is, imagine the length of 94 trillion football fields joined together, and then times that distance by 100 billion! That is somewhere in the ballpark of how big our universe is—and Jesus is bigger than that because he is the one holding the whole universe together.[19]

---

[17] He is the image of the invisible God, the firstborn over all creation. For by him all things were created: things in heaven and on earth, visible and invisible, whether thrones or powers or rulers or authorities; all things were created by him and for him. He is before all things, and in him all things hold together. *Colossians 1:15-17*

[18] But in these last days he has spoken to us by his Son, whom he appointed heir of all things, and through whom he made the universe. *Hebrews 1:2*

[19] He who descended is the very one who ascended higher than all the heavens, in order to fill the whole universe. *Ephesians 4:10*

Although this is the vastness, strength and enormity that he possesses, approximately 2,000 years ago he gave up his divine position in the heavens, humbled himself and became not only a man, but a single seed in the womb of a woman.[20]

Jesus went from being quite literally the largest of all life forms, to the smallest of all seeds. Talk about humbling himself! Why did Jesus do that?

He did it to reveal the depths of God's love for you.[21]

A male sperm is quite literally one of the smallest living organisms in creation; one sperm is about 15 times smaller than the tip of a hair on your arm—it's incredibly tiny! That was the size Jesus was willing to become in the womb of a woman. He became a little more than nothing, so that we could become everything in the eyes of God.[22]

What no man could have ever imagined was the very thing God prepared for us; that the all powerful Son of God, who holds the whole universe together, would humble himself and come down into his creation as the tiniest of life forms, a single seed in the womb of a woman. He did this so that he could grow up amongst us, feel our burdens, experience our life, and reveal the truth about our heavenly Father.

The Son of God did not just reveal God's love through words, but ultimately through his own body and sacrifice. He let mankind

---

[20]   But when the time had fully come, God sent his Son, born of a woman, born under law, to redeem those under law, that we might receive the full rights of sons. *Galatians 4:4-5*

[21]   This is how God showed his love among us: He sent his one and only Son into the world that we might live through him. *1 John 4:9*

[22]   Your attitude should be the same as that of Christ Jesus: Who, being in very nature God, did not consider equality with God something to be grasped, but made himself nothing, taking the very nature of a servant, being made in human likeness. And being found in appearance as a man, he humbled himself and became obedient to death—even death on a cross! *Philippians 2:5-8*

reject him, mock him, torture him, and nail him to a cross. It was after mankind did all of this, while he was still hanging upon the cross that he stared heavenward to his Father and said:

Father, forgive them, for they do not know what they are doing.

Luke 23:34

> **The cross is God's way of revealing his true intentions for mankind. God's heart does not seek to condemn mankind; God's heart is for reconciliation**

How great is Christ's love for us? It is so great that even after mankind rejected him, mocked him and ultimately killed him, his heart was still longing that we receive forgiveness from God. The cross is God's way of revealing his true intentions for mankind.

God's heart does not seek to condemn mankind; his heart is for reconciliation. He longs for all mankind to know him and be reconciled to him. Jesus was the one who made the way for this to be possible. The cross is God's testimony of his radical love for us.[23]

---

[23] All this is from God, who reconciled us to himself through Christ and gave us the ministry of reconciliation: that God was reconciling the world to himself in Christ, not counting men's sins against them. And he has committed to us the message of reconciliation.
2 Corinthians 5:18-19

2   The finished work of Jesus

When he had received the drink, Jesus said, "It is finished." With that, he bowed his head and gave up his spirit

John 19:30

I find it amazing that Jesus, the almighty Son of God, would come to earth to finish something for his Father. It was a task that couldn't be finished in heaven, he actually had to come to earth to complete it.

It was a task that couldn't be done in his divinely powerful body, it had to be done in the weakness of a man's body. It was a task that wasn't completed with him sitting on an earthly throne in Jerusalem, but rather it was finished with him dying on a lonely cross outside the city.

So what exactly did Jesus finish? He explained this to his first disciples at the last supper, just before he went to the cross:

Father, the time has come. Glorify your Son, that your Son may glorify you. For you granted him authority over all people that he might give eternal life to all those you have given him. Now this is eternal life: that they may know you, the only true God, and Jesus

Christ, whom you have sent. I have brought you glory on earth by completing the work you gave me to do.

John 17:2-4

The finished work of Jesus upon the cross is what gave all of us the opportunity to take hold of *eternal life*. Eternal life is often associated with heaven, streets of gold and singing angels, but that wasn't how Jesus defined eternal life. His definition of eternal life is this: *"That they may know you, the only true God"*.

Jesus' death upon the cross allowed us all to see God, for the first time, as he truly is: the God who loved us so much that he was willing to allow his perfect divine Son to die for us all, that we may live with him forever![24]

Before this time, the whole world had an opinion of who God was and what he was like. Some people had a good opinion, some had a negative opinion, but ultimately nobody had the right opinion. No matter how good someone may have believed God was, they could not possibly have imagined he was *this* good.

Jesus came as a servant to the Jewish people[25], fulfilling an old covenant not one of them had ever succeeded in doing, so they could now enter the better covenant promised to them:[26] *"It is finished."*

---

[24] For God so loved the world that he gave his one and only Son, that whoever believes in him shall not perish but have eternal life. *John 3:16*

[25] For I tell you that Christ has become a servant of the Jews on behalf of God's truth, to confirm the promises made to the patriarchs. *Romans 15:8*

[26] This righteousness from God comes through faith in Jesus Christ to all who believe. There is no difference, for all have sinned and fall short of the glory of God, and are justified freely by his grace through the redemption that came by Christ Jesus. *Romans 3:22-24*

Jesus established a new covenant for both Jew and Gentile, tearing down the walls of hostility and opening up a new and living way; a new covenant of grace, apart from law:[27] *"It is finished."*

Jesus took the punishment for all our sins, all our rejection of God and all our faults, so that we could inherit the blessing of complete forgiveness and acceptance from God:[28] *"It is finished."*

> So what exactly did Jesus finish?

Jesus revealed the depths of God's love for mankind; that he so loved the world, he sent his only Son to die for us all, so that we could live with him forever:[29] *"It is finished."*

If you want to know who God truly is, just look to the cross. Take a moment to see Jesus, and *remember who he is.* He didn't have to come, but he came freely that you may know the truth about your heavenly Father. God is not angry with you, nor is he disappointed. His love for you truly knows no limits!

When we look to the cross and see the fullness of what Jesus accomplished and the fullness of whom he is, we can breathe easily, rest in his presence and joyfully declare together with our beloved Saviour: ***"It is finished."***

Seeing Jesus from heaven's perspective, we can begin to understand why his sacrifice is more than enough for our forgiveness and our new life. He didn't only give up his supremely powerful position

---

[27] Therefore no one will be declared righteous in his sight by observing the law; rather, through the law we become conscious of sin. But now a righteousness from God, apart from law, has been made known, to which the Law and the Prophets testify. *Romans 3:20-21*

[28] In him we have redemption through his blood, the forgiveness of sins, in accordance with the riches of God's grace that he lavished on us with all wisdom and understanding. *Ephesians 1:7-8*

[29] For God did not send his Son into the world to condemn the world, but to save the world through him. *John 3:17*

as the almighty Son of God when he came to earth as a son of man; he actually gave up *everything* upon the cross. He loves us so much, that upon the cross he gave up all that he was. He became like us in his death, so that through his resurrection we could become like him![30]

He was the light of the world, yet for our sake he hung in darkness upon the cross[31], so that through him we could become light in the Lord[32]. He was the righteousness of God, and for our sake became the sin of man, so that we could be holy in the eyes of God[33]. He was the life of God, and yet he tasted death, followed by judgement for the sins of the world, so that we would never have to be condemned.[34] He was innocent of any rebellion against God, yet for our sake he took the cup of God's wrath out of our hands and drank it on our behalf[35], so that we, now innocent in God's eyes, could freely drink from the cup of communion with God.[36]

He experienced all of the consequences of rebellion against God, so that we would experience all of the benefits of being God's

---

[30] We were therefore buried with him through baptism into death in order that, just as Christ was raised from the dead through the glory of the Father, we too may live a new life. If we have been united with him like this in his death, we will certainly also be united with him in his resurrection. *Romans 6:4-5*

[31] He trusts in God. Let God rescue him now if he wants him, for he said, 'I am the Son of God.' In the same way the robbers who were crucified with him also heaped insults on him. From the sixth hour until the ninth hour darkness came over all the land. *Matthew 27:43-45*

[32] For you were once darkness, but now you are light in the Lord. Live as children of light. *Ephesians 5:8*

[33] God made him who had no sin to be sin for us, so that in him we might become the righteousness of God. *2 Corinthians 5:21*

[34] But we see Jesus, who was made a little lower than the angels, now crowned with glory and honour because he suffered death, so that by the grace of God he might taste death for everyone. *Hebrews 2:9*

[35] This is what your Sovereign LORD says, your God, who defends his people: 'See, I have taken out of your hand the cup that made you stagger; from that cup, the goblet of my wrath, you will never drink again.' *Isaiah 51:22*

[36] In the same way, after supper he took the cup, saying, 'This cup is the new covenant in my blood; do this, whenever you drink it, in remembrance of me.' *1 Corinthians 11:25*

beloved children. He took every punishment, every pain, every suffering, every sin and every rebellious act against God. All of these things were nailed to Jesus as he was nailed to the cross. He took upon the cross everything that could ever separate us from God, so that we could have confidence in being united with God for all of eternity.[37]

The reason we qualify to be radically loved is not because we have earned it by our own efforts, it is because Christ has qualified for us. Jesus did it all. This is the finished work of Christ. This is the perfect picture of God's grace for our lives.

The cross reveals why we can trust that his grace for our lives is sufficient. It is what our entire walk of faith is founded upon. We do not spend our lives trying to finish God's work; we rest in the knowledge that Jesus has finished everything on our behalf. It is this revelation that allows us to live as we truly are: *free from sin and free from religious obligations—free to live a life of love.*

Jesus is the reason that we can walk our journey of faith with this heavenly mindset[38], and not be burdened by a religious mindset of spiritual debt[39]. Christ has paid for everything. As far as God is concerned, all debts owed to him have been paid. Because of this, we can have peace before him. When we feel that we still owe God, we can not rest in his presence. Instead, we forever try to pay off our debt to him through spiritual disciplines, and in the process fail miserably to live up to our own religious standards.

---

[37]   Once you were alienated from God and were enemies in your minds because of your evil behaviour. But now he has reconciled you by Christ's physical body through death to present you holy in his sight, without blemish and free from accusation. *Colossians 1:21-22*

[38]   Since, then, you have been raised with Christ, set your hearts on things above, where Christ is seated at the right hand of God. *Colossians 3:1*

[39]   It is for freedom that Christ has set us free. Stand firm, then, and do not let yourselves be burdened again by a yoke of slavery. *Galatians 5:1*

In Christ you can be assured God is not relating to you based on how much you pray or read your Bible. He is not counting how many people you share your faith with, nor how much money you give away. Naturally in our journey of faith we may do these things, however they are not an obligation or God's measuring stick regarding your spiritual condition. They are simply a response to the reality of our salvation.

God is always speaking to you with love, and reminding you of Jesus; the one who paid the debt on your behalf. God wants you to rest in his presence with the knowledge that Christ has made you acceptable before him in every way.

Jesus is the reason we can confidently accept every blessing God pours out upon us. Everything is given freely to us, because of what he has done on our behalf.

When we live with the revelation of his finished work, the power of God moves radically in us, and that same power outworks his will in our lives. That great power is Christ himself, for he is in us, and he is our hope of glory![40]

Praise Jesus, for he is worthy. He laid down everything, that we may be given everything. He became the son of man, so that by grace we could become sons of God.

---

[40]   To them God has chosen to make known among the Gentiles the glorious riches of this mystery, which is Christ in you, the hope of glory. *Colossians 1:27*

3   The confused disciples

They kept asking, 'What does he mean by 'a little while'? We don't understand what he is saying.'

John 16:18

When we look into the gospels we find something very interesting about the disciples. We find that they really wanted to follow Jesus. They really wanted to be great men of God. They really wanted to do whatever it took to please him. Their hearts' desire was honourable; however, the problem was that they almost always misunderstood the actual purpose of everything Jesus did![41]

When we read through the gospels we find over and over again how Jesus did something, but the disciples didn't understand him. He said something, but the disciples interpreted his words to mean something else. He meant one thing, but the disciples thought he meant something else.[42]

---

[41] The disciples did not understand any of this. Its meaning was hidden from them, and they did not know what he was talking about. *Luke 18:34*

[42] Aware of their discussion, Jesus asked, 'You of little faith, why are you talking among yourselves about having no bread? Do you still not understand? Don't you remember the five loaves for the five thousand, and how many basketfuls you gathered? Or the seven

There is no doubt the disciples genuinely wanted to follow him, it just seemed that they were always looking at things from the wrong perspective. They spent most of the time looking at Jesus, his mission, as well as their purpose as disciples through the filter of their own religious ideas and traditions, instead of through the eyes of his grace. As we reflect on the gospels we begin to see just how often the disciples missed the point![43]

> The disciples spent most of the time looking at Jesus, his mission, as well as their purpose as disciples through the filter of their own religious ideas and traditions, instead of through the eyes of his grace

Seeing the shaky walk of faith that the early disciples had can be somewhat comforting to us as believers. If the disciples, who actually walked with Jesus, didn't understand him immediately, but went on a journey that lasted their whole lives, then it is OK if we also don't already have everything figured out yet in our walk with Jesus.

It is a comfort to us to know that we too, like the disciples, are really genuine in our devotion to Christ. However, just like the disciples, we sometimes misunderstand him; we sometimes allow our religious baggage to direct our understanding, instead of allowing his grace to be our guide.[44] In a moment of honesty we may even find ourselves admitting we spend more time focused on ourselves,

---

loaves for the four thousand, and how many basketfuls you gathered? How is it you don't understand that I was not talking to you about bread?' *Matthew 16:8-11*

[43] Then Jesus said to them, 'Don't you understand this parable? How then will you understand any parable?' *Mark 4:13*

[44] Now then, why do you try to test God by putting on the necks of the disciples a yoke that neither we nor our fathers have been able to bear? No! We believe it is through the grace of our Lord Jesus that we are saved, just as they are. *Acts 15:10-11*

or our programs and ministries, than we spend simply enjoying the wonderful reality that we belong to him.

Although we can drift into a mindset of works and religious obligations, God is always gracious to us, and he continues to draw us back to the truth through his kindness and patience.

Walking with Jesus is a journey of faith that involves acknowledging that we don't know as much as we thought we knew. It is a journey of sometimes making mistakes and unintentionally misunderstanding him. Jesus does not desire to see his disciples confused; he desires to see us truly free. To move from confusion to clarity in our walk with Jesus does not require more self-effort; it requires seeing more of his greatness.

At times, following him can be a journey that includes making mistakes, and that's OK with God. He understands and he cares. He does not expect us to do it alone; he has given us the Holy Spirit as our guide, who desires to pour heavenly revelation into our hearts regarding Christ's greatness and his eternal covenant, established by God's grace.[45]

---

45 I have much more to say to you, more than you can now bear. But when he, the Spirit of truth, comes, he will guide you into all truth. He will not speak on his own; he will speak only what he hears, and he will tell you what is yet to come. He will bring glory to me by taking from what is mine and making it known to you. *John 16:12-14*

4 No condemnation

Therefore, there is now no condemnation for those who are in Christ Jesus.

Romans 8:1

The journey of walking with Jesus is one that involves no condemnation because Christ paid for all of our mistakes and carried all of our condemnation on the cross. The more time that we spend beholding him and allowing the Holy Spirit to teach us of his greatness and of his perfect finished work upon the cross, the more we are transformed along the way. We can rest in the truth that we don't need to be perfect in our own strength, we just need to rest in the truth that God considers us perfectly acceptable because we believe upon his Son.

We can walk this great journey without fear or condemnation because as we walk, we rely on God's grace and not on our perfect steps. When we fall, we know Christ will always be there to pick us up, not with a condemning word, but with a confirming word of his grace. Christ cares for us, and he has sent the Holy Spirit into our hearts to remind us that we are perfect in him and are loved as precious children in the eyes of God our Father![46]

> The religious world may want to drag you before God for judgement, but God's desire is to justify you by his grace. Christ is not a condemner, he is a life giver!

Jesus is a great King, and it is his grace that empowers us to be able to live a life that can leave sin behind us and enable us to walk in his ways of love. The religious world may want to drag you before God for judgement, but God's desire is to justify you by his grace. Christ is not a condemner, he is a life giver![47]

As disciples who have been justified by Christ's perfect finished work upon the cross, we now share in the joy of listening to the Holy Spirit in our lives. The Holy Spirit has been given to us to live with us and to remind us that we are children of God. We only need to give ourselves permission to hear the life-giving words that the Holy Spirit is saying to us today, for the Holy Spirit is testifying to our spirit daily that we are God's beloved children![48]

---

[46] Jesus straightened up and asked her, 'Woman, where are they? Has no one condemned you?' 'No one, sir,' she said. 'Then neither do I condemn you,' Jesus declared. 'Go now and leave your life of sin.' *John 8:10-11*

[47] For God did not send his Son into the world to condemn the world, but to save the world through him. *John 3:17*

[48] For you did not receive a spirit that makes you a slave again to fear, but you received the Spirit of sonship. And by him we cry, 'Abba, Father.' The Spirit himself testifies with our spirit that we are God's children. *Romans 8:15-16*

5   The self-focused disciples

Jesus replied, 'You do not realize now what I am doing, but later you will understand.'

John 13:7

How could the twelve disciples walk with Jesus, spend every day with him, and still misunderstand him and his message? It was possible because during the time that they walked with him they didn't have the revelation of the almighty power of Christ's cross. The cross is what changed everything.

The disciples in the gospel accounts did not realise God's greater purpose. They were focused on what, according to their religious upbringing, they believed the Christ would accomplish in regards to their worldly external situation. God's actual plan, to make them a new creation through the finished work of Christ with a new covenant and a new spiritual reality, was a foreign concept to them. Before the reality of the cross was revealed to the disciples, they were focused more on how they could be great disciples of God, how they could improve their own faith and what they could do to be considered great in God's eyes.

It's interesting to note that even eight years after the resurrection of Jesus, the Apostles still did not understand that the new covenant was available to Gentiles![49] They still believed it was an exclusive covenant only to the Jews. This is not the only time in the Scriptures that we see how the Apostles did not understand the fullness of God's grace. In fact, the whole book of Acts reveals to us how the Apostles went on a journey of growing in their understanding of the new covenant reality and the power and greatness of the grace of God.[50]

Seeing this situation in the gospel accounts helps us as disciples today to understand the necessity of being conscious of the true purpose of Christ. Even if we are so zealous for Jesus that we give up everything to follow him as the original twelve disciples did, without a revelation of his finished work we will end up zealously trying to finish God's work, misunderstanding God's purposes and burning out along the way.[51]

Today there are many Christians that are zealous for God, but that do not understand the reality of what Christ accomplished upon the cross. Without a revelation of his finished work, a believer will naturally wander back into a religious 'works orientated' mindset. This mindset makes a disciple look at their own ideas (when

---

[49]   The apostles and the brothers throughout Judea heard that the Gentiles also had received the word of God. So when Peter went up to Jerusalem, the circumcised believers criticized him and said, 'You went into the house of uncircumcised men and ate with them'. Peter began to explain everything to them precisely as it happened. 'So if God gave them the same gift as he gave us, who believed in the Lord Jesus Christ, who was I to think that I could oppose God?' When they heard this, they had no further objections and praised God, saying, 'So then, God has granted even the Gentiles repentance unto life.' *Acts 11:1-18*

[50]   At first his disciples did not understand all this. Only after Jesus was glorified did they realize that these things had been written about him and that they had done these things to him. *John 12:16*

[51]   For I can testify about them that they are zealous for God, but their zeal is not based on knowledge. Since they did not know the righteousness that comes from God and sought to establish their own, they did not submit to God's righteousness. *Romans 10:2-3*

they should be looking at the cross) to understand the scriptures, God, the gospel, their identity and their worth.

This perspective can lead believers to either harden their hearts to God's grace, or have an overwhelming feeling of spiritual inadequacy. When we see the fullness of what Christ has accomplished for us, we begin to see all things according to his grace and we finally begin to rest in his presence.

6   The new creation

Therefore if anyone is in Christ, he is a new creation; the old has gone, the new has come!

2 Corinthians 5:17

It's so good to know that when we accept Christ as our Lord and Saviour, God makes us a new creation in him. God doesn't try to fix the old you; he makes you completely new in Christ! It really is good news for our lives. The word 'gospel' literally means 'good news'. The good news of Jesus Christ is that through faith in him we are made a new creation and are given a new life.

The message of forgiveness through Jesus is a very significant part of the message; however, it is so important to recognise that it is not the full message. There is more good news within the good news! The gospel is the good news of the new covenant in which there is forgiveness of sins and also new life. When the angel of the Lord freed the Apostles from prison he said to them:

Go, stand in the temple courts and tell the people the full message of new life!

Acts 5:20

Up to this point, the Apostles were only preaching the good news of the forgiveness of sins, however, now the Lord was encouraging them to start preaching the full message of new life. New creation life in Jesus!

In him you have not only been saved but you have also been made a new creation, with a new reality and new found blessings and privileges. God knew that if he had to fix the *old you* it would have taken him the rest of eternity, and he simply couldn't wait that long to pour out his unfailing love upon you. This is why he made you *a new creation*, so that there would be nothing in you that could separate you from the love of Christ.[52]

> When you accepted Christ, your reality changed.

Being made a new creation does not mean that we will now freely indulge in the sinful nature without any consequences. What it means is that a new reality has been given to us by which we are no longer trapped by sin.[53] When you accepted Christ, your reality changed.[54] Now that you are a new creation in him, you have been born again, no longer with the nature of Adam, but now with the nature of Christ! This means that you no longer sin by nature, but you now live a righteous life by nature.[55]

---

[52] Who shall separate us from the love of Christ? Shall trouble or hardship or persecution or famine or nakedness or danger or sword? As it is written: 'For your sake we face death all day long; we are considered as sheep to be slaughtered.' No, in all these things we are more than conquerors through him who loved us. For I am convinced that neither death nor life, neither angels nor demons, neither the present nor the future, nor any powers, neither height nor depth, nor anything else in all creation, will be able to separate us from the love of God that is in Christ Jesus our Lord. *Romans 8:35-39*

[53] You, my brothers, were called to be free. But do not use your freedom to indulge the sinful nature; rather, serve one another in love. *Galatians 5:13*

[54] Therefore, if anyone is in Christ, he is a new creation; the old has gone, the new has come! *2 Corinthians 5:17*

[55] But the gift is not like the trespass. For if the many died by the trespass of the one man, how much more did God's grace and the gift that came by the grace of the one man, Jesus Christ, overflow to the many! Again, the gift of God is not like the result of the one man's

As a new creation in Jesus, the 'sin man', who led us to live sinfully, has been condemned at the cross with Jesus, and now as a new creation you have the 'righteous man' living in you—that is Christ in you.[56] In fact, the Scriptures say that when you were 'in Adam' you were controlled by sin, but now that you are 'in Christ' you are controlled by righteousness. You are now controlled by Christ in you, who is leading you in his ways![57]

---

sin: The judgment followed one sin and brought condemnation, but the gift followed many trespasses and brought justification. For if, by the trespass of the one man, death reigned through that one man, how much more will those who receive God's abundant provision of grace and of the gift of righteousness reign in life through the one man, Jesus Christ. *Romans 5:15-17*

[56] For what the law was powerless to do in that it was weakened by the sinful nature, God did by sending his own Son in the likeness of sinful man to be a sin offering. And so he condemned sin in sinful man. *Romans 8:3*

[57] You have been set free from sin and have become slaves to righteousness. *Romans 6:18*

7   The old and the new

Do not lie to each other, since you have taken off your old self with its practices and have put on the new self, which is being renewed in knowledge in the image of its Creator.

Colossians 3:9-10

As a believer, it is so important to actually believe the reality of what Christ has done on your behalf. He has really made you into a new creation. You really are now a saint. You really do have a righteous nature! Christ really did cut away your sinful nature[58] so that you can now freely live with him and for him. All of this was not the fruit of your work, but the fruit of Christ's perfect finished work upon the cross.

Whenever we look at ourselves apart from the revelation of the cross, we can not see the reality of our new selves. This results in holding on to a religious mindset that believes that we are still the same people we were before we accepted him. When we continue to believe that we are our old selves, then our old mindsets,

---

[58]   In him you were also circumcised, in the putting off of the sinful nature, not with a circumcision done by the hands of men but with the circumcision done by Christ.
Colossians 2:11

our old ideas about God and ultimately our old sinful practices begin to reflect this belief.

The old self is naturally spiritually inadequate because it was made through the body of Adam, the original sinner. However, the truth is that we are no longer the old self; we have been made into a new creation.

We were all born the first time through the body of Adam, but through our faith we have been born again spiritually through the body of Christ. He is not like Adam, he is not a sinner. Adam may have passed on the nature of sin, but Christ is the righteousness of God, and it is this nature that he passes on to all who are born through him!

Now if we believe that the old self was sinful, how much more should we believe that the new self is righteous? Think about it, if Adam's sin was powerful enough to make all mankind sinful, how much more is Christ's righteousness powerful enough to make all who are in him righteous?[59]

Now that we are in Christ, it is so important to believe the right things regarding both our true identity in him, and how God is now relating to us based on this reality. He relates to us based on the righteousness of Christ, not the sin of Adam. In fact, it is only through focusing fully on the work that Christ completed through the cross that we can have the confidence to believe it!

---

[59]   But the gift is not like the trespass. For if the many died by the trespass of the one man, how much more did God's grace and the gift that came by the grace of the one man, Jesus Christ, overflow to the many! Again, the gift of God is not like the result of the one man's sin: The judgment followed one sin and brought condemnation, but the gift followed many trespasses and brought justification. For if, by the trespass of the one man, death reigned through that one man, how much more will those who receive God's abundant provision of grace and of the gift of righteousness reign in life through the one man, Jesus Christ. **Romans 5:15-17**

It is the glorious news that we are a new creation, made perfect by faith in the eyes of God. We are not only adequate in our relationship with him, but we also qualify, based on Christ qualifying on our behalf, to be citizens of heaven.[60]

So now we are in the new covenant of grace, but what about the old covenant of law? Some believers might argue that the law is still applicable and essential to Christian living because it helps us know the way in which we should live, but is that really true? Some may genuinely ask: "how we will know what is good from bad without the law? How will we know what God expects from us without the law? How will we live a moral life without the law? How will we know the way God wants us to walk without the law to show us the way?"

> Now if we believe that the old self was sinful, how much more should we believe that the new self is righteous?

The Apostle Thomas had a very similar thought. At the last supper Jesus said:

> 'You know the way to the place where I am going.' Thomas replied 'Lord, we don't even know where you are going, so how can we know the way?'
>
> *John 14:4-5*

Thomas had a very sincere question. He was basically asking Jesus how they would ever be able to know the way if they didn't have a map or written directions?

---

[60] Give thanks to the Father, who has qualified you to share in the inheritance of the saints in the kingdom of light. For he has rescued us from the dominion of darkness and brought us into the kingdom of the Son he loves. *Colossians 1:12-13*

What was Jesus' response to Thomas? Did he say, "You know the way because you have been instructed by the law?" Or did he say, "You know the way because you have the Ten Commandments to guide you?" If not, then what did he say? He answered:

'I am the way.'

As Christians, we know the way to live, because we are led by, and are living in, *'the way'* himself! The Holy Spirit is not just a nice idea, he is real! One thing is for certain: *When we do our part, he does his!* Our part is to look to Christ for our justification before God, and the Holy Spirit's part is to bring about the transformational life.

You can't go the *wrong way* by putting all your confidence in Jesus and the fullness of his grace, because *he is the way!* It is when we try *to find the way* by following a written code that we actually lose our way, because our focus is no longer on our glorious Saviour, but our own failed attempt at legalistic righteousness.

Christ loves God's ways, and he loves to see his beloved living in God's ways. Christ also knows that this will only come to pass if we can look to him alone. Complete dependence on the Spirit of Christ to lead us is what brings about a transformed life! The Apostle Paul also testifies to this wonderful truth:

For what the law was powerless to do in that it was weakened by the sinful nature, God did by sending his own Son in the likeness of sinful man to be a sin offering. And so he condemned sin in sinful man, in order that the righteous requirements of the law might be fully met in us, who do not live according to the sinful nature but according to the Spirit.

Romans 8:3-4

Anything that is loving and moral and good is from God, and we can rest assured that these good qualities will bear fruit in our lives by the power of the Spirit without ever seeking direction or help from the law.

Why can we say with confidence, as Paul did, that Christ is the end of the law for all who believe?[61] Because now that we see Jesus, we see the power of his life and understand that his powerful life is now living in us!

The law was never the saviour of wicked mankind; it was given to mankind that we might find the Saviour. Now that we have found him, let us believe him when he says *'I am the way'* and follow without looking back to the law.

Living in the new covenant of God's grace and being led by the Spirit isn't a licence for immorality. It is freedom to let Christ transform your life by the working of his Spirit in you. Praise God.

---

[61]   Christ is the end of the law so that there may be righteousness for everyone who believes. *Romans 10:4*

8　It's good news!

We tell you the good news: What God promised our fathers he has fulfilled for us, their children, by raising up Jesus.

Acts 13:32-33

How good is our God, that he would give us such good news? He has done everything on our behalf. He has prepared the way for us to come freely before him with freedom and confidence. He has given us everything, and we now freely thank him for his grace and his unfailing love. We only need to believe upon Jesus for whom he truly is and our works obligation to God is perfectly fulfilled. No wonder God calls it good news for mankind!

Some may still ask, "How can that be enough?" Some may argue that there is still so much to be done in the world and so much to be done in the life of the believer. Yes, that is true, but again we need to remember how all of these things are accomplished. Are they done by our own will and zeal? No, they are not! They are done by the grace of God working in us. They are done by the transformational power of the Spirit of God.[62]

The grace and Spirit of God operate in our lives when we have our eyes fixed on the greatness of Jesus[63]. You need to remember that the fruit of the Spirit is exactly that. It is the fruit of the 'Spirit'; it is not the fruit of 'you'. The Spirit needs to produce the fruit in you.

You don't need to tell an apple tree to produce apples. The fact that it is an apple tree means that by its very nature it will produce apples. Why? Because it is an apple tree, that's what it has been created to do!

We have been made a new creation in Christ and now God calls us a righteous branch connected to Christ, our righteous tree! Because we are a part of the righteous tree, guess what fruit we produce? That's right, we produce the fruit of righteousness.

As Christians, we don't need to be taught the basic 'right and wrongs' of the world; we need to be taught about the greatness of our King. When Jesus is lifted up in our meetings and in our teachings, the Spirit of God can and will transform us. The Spirit will produce its own fruit in our lives.

If you are in Christ then you can rest assured that your life will produce the fruit that God desires and can rest in him with assurance that his grace is sufficient for your life. If you are in Christ, then you are a branch connected to a very good tree, to Christ himself! So if you are now a good tree in the Lord then you know with

---

[62] But by the grace of God I am what I am, and his grace to me was not without effect. No, I worked harder than all of them—yet not I, but the grace of God that was with me. *1 Corinthians 15:10*

[63] And we, who with unveiled faces all reflect the Lord's glory, are being transformed into his likeness with ever-increasing glory, which comes from the Lord, who is the Spirit. *2 Corinthians 3:18*

assurance that Christ will produce much good fruit in and through your life.[64]

Even if we wanted to produce fruit of the Spirit in our own strength, Jesus has told us that we can't. It's only by his power working in us that good fruit is produced. Our job is to believe, God's job is to transform. Our job is to believe, God's job is to produce the good fruit in our lives by his Spirit. We don't need to desperately try to produce spiritual apples! It is the blessing of God over our lives that allows us to rest in the truth that Christ in us is the spiritual fruit maker in our lives.[65]

---

[64]   No good tree can bear bad fruit, nor does a bad tree produce good fruit. Each tree is recognised by its fruit. *Luke 6:43-44*

[65]   I am the vine; you are the branches. If a man remains in me and I in him, he will bear much fruit; apart from me you can do nothing. *John 15:5*

9 The 'Jesus answer' regarding God's work

What must we do to do the works God requires?

John 6:28

When Jesus walked the earth the people came to him in search of an answer. They all had the same question that burned in their hearts. They wanted to know from him what God required from them. They desperately wanted an answer as to their question: *"What must we do to do the works God requires?"*

It's a good question they asked, a very important question actually. Our whole walk of faith depends on the answer to this question. So, what is the answer? What works do we have to do for God? What does he require from us? Jesus gave the people this answer:

The work of God is this: to believe in the one he has sent.

John 6:29

Isn't that an amazing answer? According to Jesus, the work our heavenly Father requires from us is to simply believe upon him, that's it! You are to believe upon the reality of whom Jesus is, and trust in him. That focus won't cause you to have an unproductive life; it is the starting point where everything happens! The power that is needed for God to accomplish many great things in and through your life is found in your belief upon his Son.

When we live by faith in who Jesus is and that we belong to him, it allows us to rest in our spirit. It is when *our* spirits are at rest in his grace that *his* Spirit is at work in us! We need to remain in the knowledge that *'it is no longer I who lives, but Christ who lives in me'*.[66] Our work is to believe, and it is the work of the Holy Spirit in our lives to move powerfully on our behalf. Without striving we are filled with hope, joy and peace. We are not just filled, but God promises to make his hope overflow in us.[67]

> **It is when *our* spirits are at rest in his grace that *his* Spirit is at work in us!**

It's good to give Christ the credit he deserves. We can sometimes fool ourselves into believing he expects so much from us, when he only asks us to do one thing—believe. If you do this one thing right, Christ in you will do everything else right on your behalf. You will be filled with the fruit of the Spirit, he will accomplish good works in you, and you will be able to give all the credit to Jesus.

We see an example of this heavenly truth in the gospel story of two disciples named Mary and Martha. Martha was working so hard to please Jesus while Mary was just sitting at his feet giving him her full attention. Martha got mad and came to the Lord to criticize Mary, and how did Jesus respond?

'Martha, Martha,' the Lord answered, 'you are worried and upset

---

[66] I have been crucified with Christ and I no longer live, but Christ lives in me. The life I live in the body, I live by faith in the Son of God, who loved me and gave himself for me. *Galatians 2:20*

[67] May the God of hope fill you with all joy and peace as you trust in him, so that you may overflow with hope by the power of the Holy Spirit. *Romans 15:13*

about many things, but only one thing is needed. Mary has chosen
what is better, and it will not be taken away from her.'

Luke 10:41-42

Don't fool yourself into thinking Jesus wants you to fill your
life up with 'ministry works' in order to please him. He would much
rather you simply sit at his feet and trust in him. Mary did the right
thing; she wanted to see the reality of Jesus. Later in the gospel
account, we see that it was Mary who understood he was going to
die upon the cross when all the other disciples were still 'self' focused and could not understand what was really going on.

It was Mary who prepared him for his burial by pouring perfume on his feet while the other disciples complained about money
being wasted. Mary was not trying to be someone great, but Jesus
was so impressed with her simple faith that he declared wherever
the gospel would be preached people would remember her as an
example of great faith![68] Her example is one of belief. She was not
trying to work for him in order to please him; rather, she rested in
his presence with joy and thankfulness. Martha thought Mary was
simply being lazy, but Jesus explained that Mary was doing exactly
what God desired.

When you allow yourself to rest at the feet of Jesus and enjoy
his company, you will always end up outworking God's will in your
life because the Spirit is free to move in you as he desires. It's a
great deal God makes with us. As we trust in him, he does all of the
work in and through us. We receive all of the benefits of a transformed life and we can then give him all of the credit with joyful
hearts.

No wonder the gospel is called the good news!

---

[68] She did what she could. She poured perfume on my body beforehand to prepare for my
burial. I tell you the truth, wherever the gospel is preached throughout the world, what
she has done will also be told, in memory of her. **Mark 14:8-9**

10   The wrong focus

At that time the disciples came to Jesus and asked, 'Who is the greatest in the kingdom of heaven?'

Matthew 18:1

When we look into the gospels, we find one major theme that continually caused arguments among the disciples, one thing they argued about that caused division amongst themselves more than anything else. What was this one thing? It was the argument about which one of them would be considered the greatest disciple!

The disciples seemed to argue a lot with other groups. They spent time arguing with the Pharisees and at other times they argued with the general public. However, it seems the only time they argued among themselves was when they argued about which one of them was the greatest.[69]

What does it mean when the Scriptures tell us the disciples were arguing about who among them was the greatest? Were the

---

[69]   They came to Capernaum. When he was in the house, he asked them, 'What were you arguing about on the road?' But they kept quiet because on the way they had argued about who was the greatest. *Mark 9:33-34*

disciples acting like the famous boxer Muhammad Ali and saying to each other, *"I am the greatest. I float like a butterfly by faith; I sting like a bee by faith!"* I'm sure this is not what was happening. So then what does it mean when the Scriptures recount that they were arguing over which one was the greatest disciple? Most likely the disciples were arguing about which one of them loved Jesus the most, and pointing out their 'good works' to prove it.

You can use your imagination to see how these arguments might have started. Thomas may have started the argument by saying something like: *"I love Jesus the most because when everyone else was scared to return to Judea, I said we should go with him and die with him there!"* Then maybe Peter stood up and said: *"No, I love Jesus the most because when everyone else was scared in the boat, I got out and walked on the water for him!"* Then perhaps Andrew interrupted his brother to tell him that he was the one who convinced Peter to come and meet Jesus in the first place, proving his love was the strongest.

One by one all the disciples could have boasted in their love for Jesus and how their passion, commitment and zeal was greater than any of the other disciples. It's interesting that the Holy Spirit interpreted their conversation as arguing over who would be remembered as the greatest disciple.

It's easy for us to think it is a noble and good thing to boast in our zeal for Jesus, but the Holy Spirit shows us that what we might really be doing is actually boasting in our own greatness. Boasting in how much we love him comes out of being 'self-focused' in our faith. It is when we turn our eyes upon Jesus and become 'Christ-focused' that we begin to stop boasting in our love for him, and start to boast in his love for us!

As Christians, we need to recognise our boast is not meant to be in how much we love Jesus, but in how much he loves us. Similarly, our focus should not be in how much we are doing for him, but in how much he has done for us.

Why would you want your relationship with Jesus to be based on how much you love him? If the relationship is build on the foundation of your love, then it is broken every time you fail to love him perfectly. However, if your relationship is based on how much he loves you, as it actually is, then your relationship with him is never broken because although you may fail the Lord, he will never fail you. This is the true foundation God wants you to build your relationship with Jesus upon. It is one that will allow you to walk in the blessing of full assurance of faith, because it is based on the perfect love of Christ.

> In this world we still face moments of weakness, but Christ is seated in the heavens where he is perfect in power!

In this world, we may have moments where we prove unfaithful to him, but he is never unfaithful to us. We need to praise God that he has given us a new covenant that is built on the foundation of Christ's faithfulness to us![70] When we know and believe this, we are transformed by God to be faithful, and to love him more.

God, in his wisdom, makes the levels in which we are transformed in our walk with him dependent on how much we fix our eyes on Jesus and give him the credit he deserves. If you really want God to transform your life, be devoted to the truth that Christ is more than enough for your transformation.

As Christians, we need to understand that our faith rests on the foundation of Christ's faithfulness to his people, not on our

---

[70] And so we know and rely on the love God has for us. God is love. Whoever lives in love lives in God, and God in him. *1 John 4:16*

faithfulness to him. I am not saying we should be unfaithful, I'm just stating the fact that while we are in this world there will be times when we fail God to some degree. In this world we still face moments of weakness, but Christ is seated in the heavens where he is perfect in power![71] It is God, who reigns supreme in the heavens, who is perfectly secure in his devotion to us.

It is good news indeed to know that when we accepted Jesus as our Lord and Saviour we were placed 'in Christ', and in him God's unfailing love for us is secure on every side. In Christ we can rest assured that God will never leave us nor forsake us, that he will always have unfailing love and kindness for us, not because we are perfect people, but because we belong to his Son.

---

[71]   The Son is the radiance of God's glory and the exact representation of his being, sustaining all things by his powerful word. After he had provided purification for sins, he sat down at the right hand of the Majesty in heaven. *Hebrews 1:3*

11 The modern day 'greatness debate'

Also a dispute arose among them as to which of them was considered to be greatest.

Luke 22:24

Which one of us is the greatest? This question is one of the driving forces behind division in the body of Christ today. Is our denomination the greatest? Is our church the greatest? Is our preacher the greatest? Is our ministry the greatest? When we focus attention on ourselves, the result is no longer a boast in Christ, but in our own accomplishments, efforts and spiritual superiority. The result is a confidence in our works, instead of a confidence in the finished work of Christ.

Our boast should not be in how our 'church' is doing a greater work than other churches are, or how our preacher is a better communicator than other preachers are. When we do this, we are simply boasting in our own greatness. When we lift up our own greatness, the result is division within the body of Christ. Of course we don't use the word 'greatness', we prefer to use words like 'passionate' or 'committed' or 'on fire', but it can so easily come back to proving our greatness in the end.

What the disciples needed to learn, is the same lesson we also need to learn—it is not our greatness that should be our focus, it is his greatness. Our focus is not meant to be our good works and how we are more 'spiritual' or more 'on fire' than other Christians; our focus is meant to be on Christ's perfect finished work that he accomplished for all of us upon the cross.

When we read Paul's letter to the Corinthians we find that many members of the church were divided among themselves. Their division originated out of their arguments over which preacher they should follow and which one they felt was the greatest. He explained to the Corinthians that their focus was on the wrong person.

Is Christ divided? Was Paul crucified for you? Were you baptized into the name of Paul?

1 Corinthians 1:13

Paul explained that no man, no preacher, including himself, was crucified for them, but Jesus was! He reminded them that they should not be trying to uphold the greatness of Paul, or any other leader in the body of Christ, but the greatness of Jesus. He said this because he knew that if the church was focused on the greatness of the preacher (or a ministry, or a denomination or anything else within the Christian framework) then they would always be divided, but if they focused on the greatness of Christ they would once again be united in love.[72]

---

[72]   If you have any encouragement from being united with Christ, if any comfort from his love, if any fellowship with his Spirit, if any tenderness and compassion, then make my joy complete by being like-minded, having the same love, being one in spirit and purpose. *Philippians 2:1-2*

When we focus on our group's greatness for God, it ultimately results in causing division in the body of Christ. This division does not arise because we don't particularly like other Christians or their ministries, but more shockingly, it is because we are indifferent about the whole thing. We just don't care. We can become so focused on our own church programs and ministries that we don't even notice if we are united with other Christians or not.

When we live like this, our Christian walk becomes burdensome and mundane. However, when we can take our eyes off of ourselves, and fix them once again upon Jesus, the result is glorious. We actually start having the desire to know our fellow brothers and sisters in Christ regardless of any program or particular movement.

When we keep our eyes on the greatness of Christ, our faith stops being about 'the programs we are in' and starts to be about 'the Christ we are in'! We feel the bond of peace with all who have a love for Christ. When Christ is our focus then our heart's desire can finally become a reality: *The body of Christ being perfectly united in love.* It is our awe of Christ and seeing the fullness of who he is in our lives that brings unity, and the Holy Spirit also gives us a supernatural love for each other.[73]

If you desire to see the body of Christ come together through being united in love, start by doing your part. Give up searching for your greatness in the Kingdom of God, and start searching to understand the greatness of Jesus. If you can do this, God will not only transform your life, he will fill you with all of his love, faith and

---

[73]   May the Lord make your love increase and overflow for each other and for everyone else, just as ours does for you. *1 Thessalonians 3:12*

grace. From God's perspective you are already great because you are his child. What could be greater than that?[74]

How great is the love the Father has lavished on us, that we should be called children of God! And that is what we are! *1 John 3:1*

12 The reed and the Rock

They all ate the same spiritual food and drank the same spiritual drink; for they drank from the spiritual rock that accompanied them, and that rock was Christ.

1 Corinthians 10:3-4

When we look once more into the gospels we see that out of all of the disciples, Peter seemed to be the stand out disciple. When his relationship with Jesus began, Jesus said something very interesting. He said to him:

Your name is Simon son of John, you will be called Peter.

John 1:42

One of the interpretations of the name Simon is 'reed'. A reed is very fragile; it is easily blown about in the wind. Peter means 'rock'. A rock is strong and solid, it stands firm. What Jesus could have been saying to him was "you are insecure and easily shaken, but I will make you stand firm." It is interesting how he interpreted that moment. Jesus meant that he was going to make him a rock through the finished work of the cross, but he interpreted Jesus' words through the focus of 'self' and spent the rest of his walk with Jesus trying to make that word come to pass in his own strength.

From that time on Peter was always trying to be the rock for Jesus. When Jesus asked a question, it was always Peter who tried to answer it first. When Jesus was walking on the water, it was Peter who stepped out of the boat and walked on the water with Jesus. Yet, in his zeal to change himself into a rock for Jesus, he found himself time and time again failing! The more he zealously tried to be a great Christian, the more he felt he was not good enough. More than that, Jesus himself seemed to be the one who kept pointing out that he had such little faith.

'Come' he said. Then Peter got down out of the boat, walked on the water and came toward Jesus. But when he saw the wind, he was afraid and, beginning to sink cried out. 'Lord, save me!' Immediately Jesus reached out his hand and caught him. 'You of little faith' he said 'why did you doubt?'

Matthew 14:29-31

The first few steps he took when he walked on the water happened while he was looking at Jesus, but he quickly turned away from him and started looking at the wind. He became scared and began to sink. At this point Jesus reached out and saved him. In that moment Jesus made an incredible statement. He said to Peter "You of little faith, why did you doubt?"

You can just imagine Peter thinking to himself, 'little faith? Are you being serious Jesus? I have huge faith, and I just walked on water by faith. What else do you want me to do to prove to you I have faith!' However, Jesus was not asking him where his faith was to walk on water; he was asking Peter why he had such little faith to keep his focus on him.

It is easy as Christians to think that we need faith to do things, but actually faith is not needed 'for' things, it is needed 'in' Christ. We need to have faith in the greatness of Christ. We need faith to believe the fullness of what he has accomplished for us, not faith to merely do great things for him.

Peter spent three years walking with Jesus trying to change himself by his efforts and his works into the 'rock' Jesus said he would be. What he eventually discovered was that he would never become the rock Jesus called him to be by his own will. He became a rock when he gave up trying to live the life of faith in his own strength, and allowed Christ to transform him by his Spirit.

Jesus died for all of us, to guarantee we would all receive the Holy Spirit, and it is this Spirit that makes all of us firm and secure in our faith. It is a gift from God based on the perfect finished work of Christ.

We are all made rocks in Christ when we are made into new creations. God doesn't expect us to change ourselves into rocks for him; he expects us to live in the one true Rock—Jesus himself. With this focus we give access to the Spirit of God to transform us into rocks for God—*firm and secure in the covenant of grace that we have with him.*

Keep your eyes on Jesus and rest in the understanding that God will transform your life to be one that reflects his great love and grace. From God's perspective, the way to have great faith is not by doing great works for God, but through beholding the greatness of Jesus. If you do this, you can be sure that the Spirit will do his part and finish all of the good works God has prepared in advance to complete through your life.[75]

---

[75]   For we are God's workmanship, created in Christ Jesus to do good works, which God prepared in advance for us to do. *Ephesians 2:10*

13   The disciple who loved Jesus

Jesus told them 'You will all fall away, for it is written: I will strike the shepherd, and the sheep will be scattered. But after I have risen, I will go ahead of you into Galilee.'

Mark 14:27-28

During the last supper Jesus made a statement that I'm sure all of the disciples found hard to believe. He told them they all would fail him; they would all fall away from him. All of the disciples were shocked, how could they fail him when they all loved him so much? They just couldn't believe it would be possible. When Jesus said this, Peter took him aside and, in essence, agreed with him that the rest of the disciples would probably fail him, but not Peter! He said to the Lord:

'Even if all fall away, I will not.' 'I tell you the truth' Jesus answered, 'today—yes, tonight—before the rooster crows twice you yourself will disown me three times', But Peter insisted emphatically, 'even if I have to die with you, I will never disown you.' And all the others said the same.

Mark 14:29-31

Peter was boasting in how much he loved Jesus, and Jesus revealed to him that with that kind of foundation he would certainly fail him. Peter couldn't understand it, and he certainly didn't believe it. He really believed that he would never fail Jesus. He really believed that his love for Jesus was more than enough, that he would never, ever be unfaithful to him. He believed this, but when the time came, Peter, like every other disciple, did fail Jesus.

He ran away and was unfaithful to Jesus when Jesus needed him the most. What happened to Peter? He was so confident he would never fall away from his commitment to Jesus, yet just like all of the other disciples, he did fail him. Peter's dependence on his love for Jesus, instead of Jesus' love for him, actually caused him to fail Jesus in his time of need.

He not only abandoned Jesus. He went on to publicly deny him three times. You can imagine how this would have made him feel even more condemned and self-focused. He failed in his love and devotion to Jesus, and because of this he ran off and wept bitterly. When Christ died on the cross Peter was not there because he was ashamed; he felt unworthy, and he felt like a total hypocrite and a failure to God.

His focus was on how much he loved Jesus, how much he could do for him and how committed he was to him. Because this was Peter's focus when he failed, he felt he was unworthy to be in the presence of Jesus again.

As Christians, we must place your confidence in Christ's love for us, and not our own willpower to continue to love Christ. The grace and power of God only starts to truly work in us when we give up trying to be the strong and perfect ones, and we allow Christ to be the strong and perfect one in us![76]

---

[76]   But Jesus said to me, 'My grace is sufficient for you, for my power is made perfect in weakness.' Therefore I will boast all the more gladly about my weaknesses so that Christ's power may rest on me. *2 Corinthians 12:9*

14 The disciple whom Jesus loved

Near the cross of Jesus stood his mother, his mother's sister, Mary the wife of Clopas, and Mary Magdalene. When Jesus saw his mother there, and the disciple whom he loved standing nearby, he said to his mother, 'Dear woman, here is your son'.

John 19:25-26

There was also another disciple who failed Jesus that night. He too was in the garden of Gethsemane with Peter, and when Jesus was arrested he too ran off in fear and unfaithfulness. He too, in his weakness and humanity, was unfaithful to Jesus. But this disciple we know was not focused on how much he loved Jesus; his focus was on how much Jesus loved him.

The Apostle John, the author of the gospel of John, like all of us, really did love Jesus, but in contrast to Peter he didn't put his confidence in his love for Jesus. Instead, he described himself as *'the disciple whom Jesus loved'*. His focus was not on how much he loved Jesus, but on how much Jesus loved him.

John had a revelation that Christ's love for him was the foundation for their relationship. He passionately loved Jesus, just as all of us do, but that was not the foundation for his relationship with

Jesus. His focus was on the unfailing love Christ had towards him. Because of this revelation, even though he failed him in the garden, he could still be with him in his time of need upon the cross. John was the only one of the twelve disciples who was at the cross with Jesus. The others were alone, weeping and feeling condemned that they had failed him.

John failed Jesus just as Peter did. He was unfaithful to Jesus just as Peter was. Yet while Peter was away from Christ feeling unworthy and weeping bitterly, John was at the foot of the cross. After he had failed Jesus he could come straight back to the foot of the cross and still be with him because he understood that his relationship with Jesus was not based on how much he loved Jesus, but on how much Jesus loved him. He understood the reason he could still be in Jesus presence was because his relationship with Jesus was not based on his faithfulness to him, it was based on Jesus' faithfulness to him, and Jesus never fails us!

> We all need to have the revelation that we the disciple Jesus lo

We all need to have the revelation that *we are the disciple Jesus loves*. When we change our boast from "I am the disciple who loves Jesus the most" to "I am the disciple whom Jesus loves" we begin to receive the freedom and joy that God has promised to us in Christ. We no longer find our boast in what we are accomplishing for Christ; instead, our boast simply becomes Christ himself!

Because of what Christ has done on our behalf we can live in God's presence with confidence, even when, in our weakness and humanity, we fail God, because we know that our relationship with

God is not based on how perfect our love is for him, but on how perfect his love is for us![77]

Peter was always trying to prove that he was the greatest disciple. Over time, he too learnt that great faith is not about our great love for Christ, but it is about Christ's great love for us. In this love we can rest with great assurance. In this love we can give God the glory that is rightfully his. In this love we can truly be free. In this love we can see Jesus for who he truly is. In this love God can transform us to love others in the same way.[78]

It's the revelation of how much Christ loves us that opens up the way for God to transform us into the great men and woman of God that we have always desired to be. We need to learn not to put our confidence in our efforts, not even it in the good things we do. As Christians, we naturally do good works, however, this is not where our confidence is placed, because the time will come when our efforts fail, and even our good works may fail, but Christ will never fail.

When we rely on our efforts to be the foundation of our relationship with Christ, we never walk our journey of faith with confidence. However when our confidence is in Christ's unfailing efforts, our walk of faith becomes one of absolute assurance!

---

[77] This is love: Not that we loved God, but that he loved us and sent his Son as an atoning sacrifice for our sins. *1 John 4:10*

[78] We love because he first loved us. *1 John 4:19*

15   It's not about me!

What has happened to all your joy?

Galatians 4:15

Sometimes we can try to transform ourselves to be better Christians; we can even try for years and still fail to see the transformation. Instead of feeling more like Christ, we feel less like him. The reason for this is because we are spending all of our time looking at ourselves, focusing on our efforts and zeal for God, and continually attempting to transform our behaviour and habits. It sounds like a noble thing to do; the problem is that it just doesn't work!

We are trying to do God's part, when God just wants us to do our part. We need to simply do our part of the deal, that is believe upon Jesus and see him for who he is. We need to look to Jesus and understand that he has made us holy not because we are perfectly holy in our flesh, but because we belong to him!

The Apostle Paul did so many great works for the Lord, but he never wanted to talk or boast in them. Paul's focus was not on his great work, it was on the greatest work ever finished, the perfect finished work of the cross. Paul was transformed into a great man of God who was used mightily by God because Paul's focus was never on himself; his eyes were always fixed upon Jesus, the author and perfecter of his faith.

> *When I came to you, brothers, I did not come with eloquence or superior wisdom as I proclaimed to you the testimony about God. For I resolved to know nothing while I was with you except Jesus Christ and him crucified.*

1 Corinthians 2:1-2

At one point in Paul's ministry he listed all of the good works he had done for the Lord.[79] He did this not to boast in himself, but to show the early church that just because he never boasted in himself, this did not mean that he had nothing he *could* boast about. He knew all of the good works that were in his life, but he also knew that compared to the blessing of knowing Christ and boasting in him, they were like rubbish.[80] He knew that when we remain Christ-focused and keep our attention on him, God will accomplish many great works through our lives.

Look to Jesus and understand that because Christ became sin upon the cross, you have now become the righteousness of God! Look to Jesus and know that every time you are temped and suffer, you can come before him with freedom and confidence because you know that he too was tempted and suffered when he walked the

---

[79] *2 Corinthians 11:16-33*

[80] If anyone else thinks he has reasons to put confidence in the flesh, I have more: circumcised on the eighth day, of the people of Israel, of the tribe of Benjamin, a Hebrew of Hebrews; in regard to the law, a Pharisee; as for zeal, persecuting the church; as for legalistic righteousness, faultless. But whatever was to my profit I now consider loss for the sake of Christ. What is more, I consider everything a loss compared to the surpassing greatness of knowing Christ Jesus my Lord, for whose sake I have lost all things. I consider them rubbish, that I may gain Christ and be found in him, not having a righteousness of my own that comes from the law, but that which is through faith in Christ—the righteousness that comes from God and is by faith. *Philippians 3:4-9*

earth.[81] Look to him and know that there is nothing you owe to God, because Christ has already paid for everything upon the cross on your behalf.

Look to him and believe that he is the reason you are blessed, not because of your performance, but because you belong to him. Look to him and understand how much it cost God to allow this to take place. God allowed his only Son to come to earth, to die for you, to pay for all of your sins, to clear your debt forever, to be resurrected in glory and now to be seated at the right hand of the Father, and what is he doing there? He is interceding in prayer for you all of the time, 24 hours a day!

> *Jesus Christ, who died—more than that, who was raised to life—is at the right hand of God and is also interceding for us.*
>
> ***Romans 8:34***

Jesus is telling the Father that you belong to him; that you are loved by him. He is asking the Father to say 'yes' to all of your prayers. He is asking the Father to favour you because you believe upon him.

Keep your eyes upon the risen Lord and boast in him and you will begin to see your life being transformed. It won't be by the power of your effort and zeal, but by the almighty power of God's Spirit! Put your confidence in the truth that Jesus is praying for

---

[81] Therefore, since we have a great high priest who has gone through the heavens, Jesus the Son of God, let us hold firmly to the faith we profess. For we do not have a high priest who is unable to sympathize with our weaknesses, but we have one who has been tempted in every way, just as we are—yet was without sin. Let us then approach the throne of grace with confidence, so that we may receive mercy and find grace to help us in our time of need. *Hebrew 4:14-16*

you. It is his prayer life and his almighty power that will bring about your transformed life.[82]

---

[82]   Because Jesus lives forever, he has a permanent priesthood. Therefore he is able to save completely those who come to God through him, because he always lives to intercede for them. *Hebrews 7:24-25*

16   Faith, Spirit, Grace and Power

This proposal pleased the whole group. They chose Stephen, a man full of faith and of the Holy Spirit... Now Stephen, a man full of God's grace and power, did great wonders and miraculous signs among the people.

Acts 6:5-8

When we read the book of Acts we find a disciple by the name of Stephen. He was such an amazing follower of Christ that the Holy Spirit introduced him twice in the space of three verses. I'm sure the Holy Spirit didn't do this because we have a very short attention span. He was introduced twice because God wanted us to pay attention to this man and learn from his life and testimony. He was introduced the first time as a man full of faith and the Holy Spirit. Three verses later he was introduced again, this time as a man full of God's grace and power!

These four characteristics that Stephen was introduced with are characteristics we all want to have, right? Most believers desire to be filled with faith, the Holy Spirit, grace and power. The Bible doesn't record that he had *some* faith, *some* Spirit, *some* grace and *some* power. The Scriptures tell us that he was *full* of each of them.

What is truly amazing is that all of these attributes that he had were gifts from God.

You can not earn more grace, it is a gift given from God, as is faith, as is God's power and as is the Holy Spirit. They are all gifts, yet the Scriptures tell us that we can be given more faith, we can be filled with more of his Spirit, we can grow in grace and we can receive more power. So the question is: *What did Stephen do to be filled to the full with each of these heavenly gifts?*

He did the one thing right; he spent his time captivated by the fullness of the Lord Jesus in all of his glory and greatness. The secret to Stephen receiving such an overflow of faith, the Holy Spirit, grace and power is that he didn't have his focus on any of these gifts; he had his focus on Jesus. He had a revelation that Jesus was more then enough for him, and because his focus was firstly on Jesus, God rewarded him with the fullness of all of these precious gifts.

Because he gave so much of his attention to Jesus and his glory, he began giving less glory to religious traditions and self-elevated 'spiritual leaders'. His faith was not controlled by men, but rather he was free in the truth of Christ. It was his love for Christ that caused the religious leaders to persecute him, as he was putting more confidence in Christ than the institution of the temple and the traditional religious customs.[83]

As he stood before the religious council to give his defence he did not just testify with his words but with his life also. His life and worldview was built upon the reality of Jesus, and it was this focus

---

[83]   So, they stirred up the crowd and produced false witnesses who testified, 'This fellow never stops speaking against this holy place and against the law. For we have heard him say that this Jesus of Nazareth will destroy this place and change the customs Moses handed down to us.' *Acts 6:12-14*

that caused him to shine with the light of Christ even while standing before his accusers!

> *All who were sitting in the Sanhedrin looked intently at Stephen, and they saw that his face was like the face of an angel.*

Acts 6:15

I'm confident that none of the members of the Sanhedrin actually knew what an angel looked like, so why did they think this? It was because when they looked into the face of Stephen they saw the radiance of God's glory reflecting off of him!

When they looked at him, it looked to them like they were staring at heaven's glory. And why was that? Because when we spend our time as Christians being captivated by the fullness of Jesus in his glory, then his glory reflects onto us and we too shine in this world with his glory. Not by our efforts, but by the work of the Spirit in us![84]

When we do the beholding, God does the transforming of our lives

He was always looking at the glorious Son of God with the eyes of faith, and the result was the Lord's glory reflecting through his life. He radiated with so much of God's glory that even those who considered themselves his enemy could see this. More than that, it allowed the Spirit to completely transform his life to be full of faith, the Holy Spirit, grace and power. All of this happened to him with ever increasing glory, not by the efforts and willpower of Stephen,

---

[84]   Now the Lord is the Spirit, and where the Spirit of the Lord is, there is freedom. And we, who with unveiled faces all reflect the Lord's glory, are being transformed into his likeness with ever-increasing glory, which comes from the Lord, who is the Spirit.
2 Corinthians 3:17-18

but by the Lord. When we do the beholding, God does the transforming of our lives![85]

He was also filled with God's wisdom. So much so that no one
could stand up against his wisdom as he proclaimed the good news
of Jesus Christ. All he wanted to do was to get people to take their
eyes off of themselves, and off of their religious bias, and look to
see Jesus for who he truly was.

Even when he finished his passionate proclamation of the gospel and the Sanhedrin still refused to acknowledge Jesus, Stephen
cried out to them all:

> 'Look,' he said, 'I see heaven open and the Son of Man standing at
> the right hand of God.'

> *Acts 7:56*

Right to the end of his life he was still captivated by Jesus. He
still had his eyes fixed on the author of his faith. Even to the end he
was still trying to get people to just look and see Jesus for who he
truly was: *The glorious Saviour of the world, now at the right hand of
God!*

When we start to see the reality of Jesus, it consumes our attention. It gives a believer such joy just to see Jesus and to see the
fullness of him. It is the greatest blessing we can have as believers:
the blessing of seeing Christ and knowing him.

Even at the point of being killed, he still tried to get people to
see Jesus for who he truly was, not their enemy, but their Saviour.
The Sanhedrin thought of Jesus as a troublemaker, because he was
messing with their religious traditions; they refused to see Jesus in
his true light, and so they thought themselves his enemy.

---

[85]   For God, who said, 'Let light shine out of darkness,' made his light shine in our hearts to
give us the light of the knowledge of the glory of God in the face of Christ.
2 Corinthians 4:6

Stephen wanted them to see the truth regarding Jesus, because he knew that if they could only see Jesus for who he truly was, they would realise that Jesus doesn't make enemies of men, he makes sons of God. Jesus doesn't make people enemies of God; he makes them friends of God. Jesus is not the one who condemns us; he is the one who saves us!

Stephen wasn't stoned for being an evil-doer; he was stoned because he was trying to point people to the righteous one. The members of the Sanhedrin refused to look, and instead picked up stones and began stoning him. Just before he died, he asked God for one final blessing. The last blessing he asked the Father for was that God would forgive the men who were stoning him!

> *Then he fell on his knees and cried out, 'Lord, do not hold this sin against them.' When he had said this, he fell asleep.*
>
> ### Acts 7:60

Who can love their enemies so much that even when they are in the middle of being killed by them, they can still ask God to forgive them? This is a supernatural love that man can not have in their own strength, but when we see the fullness of Jesus and receive him as he is, it is the kind of love Christ gives us.

Stephen did not want the sins these men committed against him to be the reason they were separated from God. He prayed that God would forgive them this sin so that they may still come to know him as their Lord and Saviour. He did this because he witnessed first hand how Christ had transformed his life. He knew that if Jesus could do it for him, he could do it for them as well, if they would only look to Jesus and see him in the fullness of his grace.

God desires to transform your life and grow the fruit of his Spirit within you. Love is not the fruit of your efforts and willpower; it is a fruit of his Spirit. Take the time to see the fullness of

Christ and God will happily transform your life by pouring out upon you the abundance of his grace.

Stephen loved abundantly and had faith in abundance because he allowed God to pour out his grace into his life in abundance. The Scriptures promise you that when you receive his grace freely, you will also receive his faith and love. They are all part of this wonderful new covenant God has made with you![86]

---

[86] The grace of our Lord was poured out on me abundantly, along with the faith and love that are in Christ Jesus. *1 Timothy 1:14*

17   Fix your eyes on Jesus

Let us fix our eyes on Jesus, the author and perfecter of our faith,
who for the joy set before him endured the cross, scorning its shame,
and sat down at the right hand of the throne of God.

Hebrews 12:2

What does the Bible mean when it encourages us to 'fix our
eyes on Jesus?' Does it mean we need to stare at a painting of Jesus
that is hanging on a wall? Of course not, so what does it mean?

Looking to Jesus is not about looking with your natural eyes,
but with the eyes of your heart. To fix your eyes on him is to believe
the reality of who he is. It is to believe what he has accomplished on
your behalf on the cross. It is to see him in your heart as your loving
redeemer. It is to communicate with him with complete assurance
based on his finished work. The apostle Paul spent his entire life
praying for, and encouraging, the early church to see Jesus with the
eyes of their hearts.

I keep asking that the God of our Lord Jesus Christ, the glorious Fa-
ther, may give you the Spirit of wisdom and revelation, so that you

may know him better. I pray also that the eyes of your heart may be
enlightened in order that you may know the hope to which he has
called you, the riches of his glorious inheritance in the saints and
his incomparably great power for us who believe.

Ephesians 1:17-19

It is not enough to just see Jesus based on our own opinions
and ideas; we need to give our heavenly Father the permission to
reveal the glorious truth of his Son to our hearts and minds. We
need to believe upon the fullness of Jesus.

When Jesus walked the earth, some saw him as a good man,
but that was not who he was. Some saw him as a prophet, but that
was not who he truly was. Some saw him as a miracle worker, but
even that was not who he truly was. Although all of these aspects
were *part* of who he was, they were not who he *truly* was.

We need to accept that Jesus is not just a good man, he is not
just a godly prophet and he is not only a miracle worker. Jesus is the
Son of God! The only one who carried our sins and pardoned us
freely. He is the one who has established a brand new covenant
between God and mankind, not based on our works but on his
grace! Until we accept the new covenant of his grace, we can never
see the full reality of Jesus.

He is the one who, by his perfect atoning sacrifice, has made us
holy and blameless in the eyes of the Father forever. He is the one
who sits at the right hand of the Father and now lives to intercede
for us.

He is the image of the invisible God, the radiance of God's
glory. He is the one who completed the perfect finished work of the
cross so that we may now be not only forgiven but also sanctified,

justified and glorified! He is the King of kings and the Lord of lords. He holds the whole universe together![87]

Jesus is united to his church in Spirit and by his grace we have become his holiness and righteousness. He is the one who is able to make men perfect before God through his perfect atoning sacrifice upon the cross. When we see him for who he truly is, in all his greatness and glory, and believe with our hearts that it is true, God gains access in our lives by this faith to do amazing things in and through us.

---

[87]   And those he predestined, he also called; those he called, he also justified; those he justified, he also glorified. What, then, shall we say in response to this? If God is for us, who can be against us? *Romans 8:30-31*

18   Who is Jesus to you?

'But what about you?' he asked. 'Who do you say I am?'

Matthew 16:15

The world may only see Jesus as a good moral teacher, and because of this never really see him at all. However, as the body of Christ, the Holy Spirit desires that we live with the revelation of his finished work fresh in our hearts and minds every day.

As Christians, we need to see him as he truly is: the reason for all of our blessings apart from our performance, the reason for all of our provision apart from our good works and the reason we can stand in the throne room of God with freedom and confidence, free from fear of judgement and condemnation.[88]

The world may be spiritually blind to this wonderful reality, but in Christ our eyes have been opened. It is in Christ that we receive our spiritual sight, and freely receive all of the treasures of wisdom that are found in him. We are blessed because we see the

---

[88]   Let us then approach the throne of grace with confidence, so that we may receive mercy and find grace to help us in our time of need. *Hebrews 4:16*

one who sets our hearts free. We see the one reflecting his glory into our lives. We see the one who gives us rest.[89]

We need to look to Jesus and not limit him to merely a moral teacher, but see him as our loving redeemer, and rest in this great assurance. When we do this, the Holy Spirit gains free access in our lives to transform us into the likeness of Christ with ever increasing glory. The likeness of Christ is a life of joy, peace, love, goodness, patience, faith, hope, security, confidence and all other heavenly attributes of the Spirit of God that are freely given to us who have faith in Christ.

It may sound noble to call Jesus a good teacher, but the truth is he is so much more

In the gospel of Mark, we read a story where Jesus himself challenged a man to not minimize who he was. The man in this story thought Jesus was a good teacher, but Jesus wouldn't accept this man's compliment. He knew better than anyone how powerful he was to save someone who believed he was the Son of God, and how useless he was to anyone who thought of him only as a good teacher.

> *As Jesus started on his way, a man ran up to him and fell on his knees before him. 'Good teacher,' he asked, 'what must I do to inherit eternal life?' 'Why do you call me good?' Jesus answered, 'No one is good—except God alone.'*
>
> **Mark 10:17-18**

It may sound noble to call Jesus a good teacher, but the truth is he is so much more. This young man was trying to point out that

---

[89] But blessed are your eyes because they see, and your ears because they hear. For I tell you the truth, many prophets and righteous men longed to see what you see but did not see it, and to hear what you hear but did not hear it. **Matthew 13:16-17**

he recognised Jesus' goodness as a teacher; Jesus wanted him to recognise his goodness as God.

At the end of this gospel story the young man went away sad because he did not receive the answer he was expecting from Jesus. He walked away disappointed and frustrated because he could only see him as a good teacher, and could not see the reality of who Jesus was.

The young man in this gospel account saw Jesus as a good man, the Pharisees saw him as a troublemaker, many other people saw him and made up their own minds regarding his identity. He watched as so many people came to listen to him, but they could not hear his true message, because they were filtering it through their own religious ideas.

When we allow our heavenly Father to reveal the true nature and identity of Jesus to our hearts, we begin to see him in a much more glorious light. We no longer see Jesus as a greater Moses with stricter rules we need to adhere to. Instead we start seeing the one who died in our place, so that we could live in his place. We see the one who fulfilled the old covenant that was based on religious obligations, to establish a new covenant that is eternally based on God's grace.

Jesus never came to make your Christian walk difficult, tiresome and burdensome; he came to give you rest. He desires to give you rest, not based on your performance in life, but because you are his beloved. Believe that God is pleased with you and accept the rest that Christ gives to those he loves.[90]

---

[90]   Come to me, all who are weary and burdened, and I will give you rest. *Matthew 11:28*

19   The true Light of the world

What does the Scripture say? 'Abraham believed God, and it was credited to him as righteousness.'

Romans 4:3

Is it really true that when we believe in Jesus, we have fulfilled our obligations to God? Is it true that by simply believing, God credits righteousness to us; not by our efforts, but by his grace?

Is the only thing that God requires from us belief upon Christ? It sounds beautiful, but how can it be true? How can just beholding Jesus with the eyes of faith be all God requires? It seems too good to be true, but I think that is exactly the point. It is too good to be true; it actually takes faith to accept it! In our rational minds it is completely unrealistic, but if we can believe it, then the power of God will prove it true in our lives.[91]

When we look at Abraham, the man of faith, what did God do with him? God gave him some good news that was totally unrealis-

---

[91]   For the message of the cross is foolishness to those who are perishing, but to us who are being saved it is the power of God. *1 Corinthians 1:18*

tic and far too good to possibly be true. Yet, in that moment Abraham did the one thing God required, he believed!

> *God took Abram outside and said 'Look up at the heavens and count the stars—if indeed you can count them.' Then he said to him, 'so shall your offspring be.' Abram believed the Lord and he credited it to him as righteousness.*
>
> ***Genesis 15:5-6***

When we look back onto this amazing moment between Abraham and God, we need to understand that it is also a moment we all share with God. Abraham's story is our story. We walk in his footsteps of faith.[92] The Apostle Paul tells us that when God spoke those words it was not meant only for Abraham, but for all of us who put our faith in Christ.

> *The words 'it was credited to him' were written not for him alone, but also for us, to whom God will credit righteousness—for us who believe in him who raised Jesus our Lord from the dead.*
>
> ***Romans 4:23-24***

The truth is God has always had Jesus on his mind. Even before the coming of Jesus, God was preparing mankind to understand him. Even before Jesus came to reveal and proclaim the gospel, the Scriptures teach us that God announced the gospel in advance to Abraham.

> *The Scripture foresaw that God would justify the Gentiles by faith, and announced the gospel in advance to Abraham: 'All nations will be blessed through you.'*
>
> ***Galatians 3:8***

---

[92]   And he is also the father of the circumcised who not only are circumcised but who also walk in the footsteps of the faith that our father Abraham had before he was circumcised. *Romans 4:12*

Have you ever wondered how God did this? How did God announce the gospel (that is, the good news of Jesus) in advance to Abraham? When we go back and read the story of Abraham's life, we find God asking Abraham to look at the stars. We also know that all Scripture finds its true meaning in Christ, as does all of creation.[93] With this in mind, what do we believe the stars represent? God tells us what they represent in the creation account in Genesis one.

> He also made the stars. God set them in the expanse of the sky to give light on the earth.
>
> **Genesis 1:16-17**

The stars were given as light to the world and they were the same stars that God asked Abraham to look to. Now we know that the true light of the world is not stars, but it is Jesus Christ himself. However, before Christ was given God used the stars to preach the gospel in advance to Abraham! We can see that God used the stars to help Abraham believe the promise of God when he was looking to the light of the world.

> The true light that gives light to every man was coming into the world.
>
> **John 1:9**

So when God asked Abraham to look to the stars and believe, he was announcing the gospel of Jesus in advance to Abraham! Stop and think about it, what did God ask Abraham to do? He asked him to look to the light of the world and believe. In doing this, God was

---

93   You diligently study the Scriptures because you think that by them you possess eternal life. These are the Scriptures that testify about me, ... *John 5:39*

proclaiming the gospel in advance to Abraham. Like Abraham, we too look to the light of the world and believe![94]

Just as the Spirit of God announced the gospel in advance to Abraham, we know that the Spirit continues to announce the gospel to all who believe upon Jesus today. God asks of this generation of believers the same thing he asked of Abraham. He asks us to look at Jesus, the true light of the world, and see all of the promises and blessings that are attributed to him. God reveals to us that through Christ and by faith in him that we have been credited with all of them. This is the reality of being a disciple of Jesus: *we have not earned any of God's promises and blessings, but God freely credits all of them to us who look to his Son and believe in him!* [95]

---

[94]   When Jesus spoke again to the people, he said, 'I am the light of the world. Whoever follows me will never walk in darkness, but will have the light of life.' *John 8:12*

[95]   For no matter how many promises God has made, they are 'Yes' in Christ. And so through him the 'Amen' is spoken by us to the glory of God. *2 Corinthians 1:20*

20 You need to see the reality

Does God give you his Spirit and work miracles among you because you observe the law, or because you believe what you heard?

Galatians 3:5

If receiving the benefits of God is meant to be so easy for us, why do many Christians still find it hard to receive them? Why do many Christians find it hard to receive the gift of righteousness, the peace of God, his promised rest and the fullness of his grace in their lives?

The main reason we still find it hard to receive the blessings of God is because we think that receiving them is based on our performance. We still fail to realise that everything is actually based on the perfect performance of Christ. Our faith is not about our performance, it is about Jesus. He has become our performance in God's eyes, and for that reason we receive all of the benefits of God through our faith in him.

When I talk about benefits, I am not talking about worldly benefits; I am talking about heavenly benefits! A person can earn money and buy things of luxury, but they can't earn the peace of God. What no one can earn, God has freely given to us! What person could ever earn the joy of God? What person could ever earn the rest of God? No one can earn these heavenly blessings, and yet through our faith in Jesus, God has freely given us all of them as a gift. We are not given the peace of God because we deserve it by our perfect life. We are given the peace of God because we belong to Christ, and he himself is our peace.[96]

We are not given the gift of righteousness because our performance has earned it, otherwise it would not be a gift but an obligation. No, it is because we believe upon Christ as our Lord and Saviour that God gives us his righteousness as a gift.

You are righteous in God's eyes not because of your performance and good works, but because you belong to Christ who is perfectly righteous. Because you are in him, God credits his righteousness to you!

We do not receive God's grace by earning it, because grace is never earned; it is God's undeserved favour. We receive grace for the very reason that we don't try to earn it, instead we believe that it is a gift to us because we believe upon Christ, the perfect Son of God.[97]

Every blessing we receive from God is given not because of our personal performance in life, but because of Christ's personal performance upon the cross. For this reason when we feel we need to earn God's blessings, it becomes impossible to receive them. We need to give up trying to earn God's favour and instead look to Jesus in all of his glory and goodness and thank God for all of his blessings that are freely given to us because we believe upon him.

---

[96]   But now in Christ Jesus you who once were far away have been brought near through the blood of Christ. For he himself is our peace. *Ephesians 2:13-15*

[97]   In him we have redemption through his blood, for forgiveness of sins, in accordance with the riches of God's grace that he lavished on us with all wisdom and understanding. *Ephesians 1:7-8*

The perfect finished work of Jesus is the basis for all of our blessings from God. Our work is to believe, and God's work is to give us every blessing as a gift. All of God's gifts are given freely to us because of our faith in Christ, his perfect Son and our perfect Saviour.[98]

When we can look to Jesus and say with our hearts "Lord I've got you, and that's enough for me," God rejoices in heaven, and because Christ is enough for us, and he is our focus and attention, God also freely gives every other heavenly blessing as well.

> **What no one can earn, God has freely given to us!**

God teaches us this great heavenly reality in the book of Kings, in the moment when God appeared to King Solomon:

> *At Gibeon the LORD appeared to Solomon during the night in a dream, and God said, 'Ask for whatever you want me to give you.'*
>
> *1 Kings 3:5*

Solomon asked for wisdom, and God got so excited he gave him not only wisdom, but also everything he didn't ask for!

> *The Lord was pleased that Solomon had asked for this. So God said to him, 'Since you have asked for this and not for long life or wealth for yourself, nor have you asked for the death of your enemies but for discernment in administering justice, I will do what you have asked. I will give you a wise and discerning heart, so that there will never have been anyone like you, nor will there ever be. Moreover, I will give you what you have not asked for—both riches and hon-our—so that in your lifetime you will have no equal among kings.'*
>
> *1 Kings 3:10-13*

---

98   He who did not spare his own Son, but gave him up for us all—how will he not also, along with him, graciously give us all things? *Romans 8:32*

Why was God so pleased that Solomon asked for wisdom before anything else? Because God knew that the reality of God's wisdom was found in his Son Jesus. God had always known that the day would come when he would send his Son to earth to become the full revelation of God's wisdom for his people!

> *But we preach Christ crucified: a stumbling block to Jews and foolishness to Gentiles, but to those whom God has called, both Jews and Greeks, Christ the power of God and the wisdom of God.*
>
> ### *1 Corinthians 1:23-24*

The Scriptures reveal a glorious gospel reality through the story of Solomon. When we desire Christ above all else, God not only gives us Christ, but freely blesses us with every other spiritual blessing. As the Apostle Paul passionately declared:

> *Praise be to the God and Father of our Lord Jesus Christ, who has blessed us in the heavenly realms with every spiritual blessing in Christ.*
>
> ### *Ephesians 1:3*

God knows that when Jesus is our one desire, God will be able to do everything he desires through us. The great thing about the good news is that it is so easy for us. God makes it so easy. He tells us that we have just one work that he requires, to believe upon the perfect finished work of Christ and to remain in him. When we do this one thing, God promises to do all of the rest of the work in and through us by the Spirit of his grace. The Holy Spirit of grace is the power to transform not just your life, but also the whole universe. His power is unlimited, and it is that power that has been placed in you!

21 Don't try to pay twice

He who did not spare his own Son, but gave him up for us all—how will he not also, along with him, graciously give us all things?

Romans 8:32

Jesus Christ did not only pay the price for all of your sins, he paid the price for all of the gifts of God in your life as well. He did it all on your behalf, and it is through accepting this wonderful reality that you can be anchored in his love and be able to freely receive the blessings of God.

If you go to a restaurant with a friend and at the end of the meal he tells you that he has already paid the bill for both of you, the result is that you have received your meal for free. It doesn't mean that your meal was not paid for in full, it just means that you personally did not have to pay for it; instead, you received it as a gift through the generosity of your friend.

In this case, even if you wanted to pay for your meal you can't because your friend has already paid for it. It would be an insult to your friend to go to the cashier and pay for your meal even though your friend had already paid for it. If you paid for it as well, the meal would have been paid for twice. Once is enough. Just accept that

Christ has already paid the full price for all of the good things God graciously gives to you and receive them thankfully as a gift.

Jesus paid for all of your forgiveness and all of your blessings. It's your job to believe that he has done it all on your behalf, and then freely receive the abundant provision of God's grace for your life. This transaction is neither based on your performance nor is it because you deserve it by your good works; rather, it is because Jesus paid for all of them on your behalf.

In the book of revelation the Apostle John recounts the time he was taken to heaven in a vision, and he recalls the song heaven was singing about Jesus:

> *And they sang a new song:*
> *'You are worthy to take the scroll*
>   *and to open its seals,*
> *because you were slain*
>   *and with your blood you purchased men for God*
>   *from every tribe and language and people and nation.*
> *You have made them to be a kingdom and priests to serve our God*
>   *and they will reign on the earth.'*
>
> ***Revelation 5: 9-10***

This is a heavenly reality that we can already outlive here on earth. Jesus is worthy by his perfect work to make us worthy by our belief in him! He has already purchased us for God, so God can now be a Father to us and pour out his blessings upon us. He has purchased us for God, so we may now reign on the earth. We can love, we can live, we can serve and we can rest because we understand the heavenly reality that we are in a perfect relationship with God.[99]

---

[99]   Since, then, you have been raised with Christ, set your hearts on things above, where Christ is seated at the right hand of God. Set your minds on things above, not on earthly things. *Colossians 3:1-2*

Praise God that we belong to such a wonderful Saviour! Boast in the greatness and the beauty and the love of Christ for our lives. Rejoice, for we are forever loved. Look to Jesus, give him the credit he deserves and praise God. Scripture tells us that we, as Christians, will reign in life because we receive the gift of his righteousness. We don't reign in life because we have earned our own righteousness, but because we receive the gift of righteousness!

Allow yourself to be righteous because you belong to him. Believe it, and thank God for this precious gift. When you can rest in the reality of your covenant relationship with him, God will transform your life through the power of his Spirit. As a result, you will see yourself living more and more in the freedom which Jesus promised by the gift of God's grace in your life.[100]

---

[100]   For if, by the trespass of the one man, death reigned through that one man, how much more will those who receive God's abundant provision of grace and of the gift of righteousness reign in life through the one man, Jesus Christ. *Romans 5:17*

22   The transformation process

Now the Lord is the Spirit, and where the Spirit of the Lord is there is freedom. And we, who with unveiled faces all reflect the Lord's glory, are being transformed into his likeness with ever-increasing glory, which comes from the Lord, who is the Spirit.

2 Corinthians 3:17-18

God is so good that he promises us that when we look to the glory of the risen Lord Jesus, that just by looking at him, his glory will be reflected in us. However, if we as Christians are not behold-ing Jesus in his glory, how can that very glory reflect into our lives?

When we are willing to just see the fullness of Jesus and the grace that is ours through him, God promises us that, by his Spirit, he will transform us more and more into the likeness of Christ. It is such a blessing to know that it is not by our efforts or will power that we are transformed into the likeness of Christ, but it is by the work of the Spirit![101]

---

[101]   For it is God who works in you to will and to act according to his good purpose. *Philippians 2:13*

It is not by our own power, but by God's own power that we are transformed into the likeness of Jesus. It is Jesus in us who produces the fruit in our lives that the Father desires. It is Jesus in us who will empower us to will and to act in accordance with God's desire.

This is such a great blessing God has given to us as believers, because if it were by our efforts and will power, then our transformation into the likeness of Christ would be very limited. But if it is by God's Spirit, by his power and by his efforts, then it is unlimited how much you and I can be transformed into the likeness of Christ. It is by the Lord, who is the Spirit, that we are being transformed with ever-increasing glory. All this is being done by God, because we did our job of looking to the greatness of Jesus!

If it was based on our efforts to be like Jesus, the truth is that none of us would ever really walk like him, or live like him. We may be able to put on a good show and look very holy once a week at a Sunday service, but we can never actually live with the love and joy that Christ demonstrated.

God is so good. He promises to us in his word that he will do the transforming in us when we simply look to the beautiful truth of who Jesus is. Our Saviour, our redeemer, our justifier who has become for us our holiness, our righteousness and our redemption! The only thing God requires from us is that we take our eyes off of ourselves and fix them upon him, the author and perfecter of our faith.

The reason that we shine with the glory of God in this world is because we behold the glorious one, and with joyful hearts say 'thank you Lord that I belong to Jesus!' God doesn't expect us to believe that we are perfect in our flesh, but he does expect us to believe that we are perfect in our spirit, because our spirit has been united to the perfect Spirit of his Son.

When God looks at you, he does not look at all of your weaknesses and your lack; he looks at your perfect belief upon his Son Jesus as your Lord and Saviour and declares that you have perfectly fulfilled all of the good work he requires from you.[102]

---

[102] Because by one sacrifice he has made perfect forever those who are being made holy. *Hebrews 10:14*

23 Heavenly results

For it is by grace you have been saved, through faith—and this not from yourselves, it is the gift of God—not by works, so that no one can boast. For we are God's workmanship, created in Christ Jesus to do good works, which God prepared in advance for us to do.

Ephesians 2:8-10

We can be assured that when we receive God's grace it won't be without effect. It will certainly bring about the Christ shining life that God intends for all of his people. Christ creates in us a desire for those things that are close to God's heart. Belonging to Christ not only gives us complete peace and assurance in God's presence, it also works in us to do all of the good work that God has already prepared in advance to do through us.

When we receive the Spirit of Christ in our hearts we don't suddenly lose all of our ability to be self-controlled, it's exactly the opposite. We need to remember that through the promise of the

Holy Spirit we are not only given a spirit of power and love, but also a spirit of self-discipline.[103]

I don't know if you have ever realised this, but 'self-control' is not a work of your efforts, it is a fruit of the Spirit. The way that you live a self-controlled life is not by focusing on yourself, it is by being focused on Christ, and by giving the Spirit of God in you permission to produce the results of self-control in your life.[104]

Those who do not have the powerful life of Christ living in them have to stress, work and beat themselves up to be self-controlled; we only need to rest in the truth. In Christ we have the blessing of being able to rest assured in his complete grace over our lives. We can rest assured of God's total love and acceptance and also rest assured that our lives will produce God's desired results. God's grace for us as believers won't lead us into ungodliness, it will actually teach us to say 'no' to ungodliness![105]

God's grace is never to be thought of as an excuse for sin, for grace is the destroyer of sin. It is through his grace, which was given to us in Christ Jesus, that sin in us was condemned. It no longer rules in us, instead, the righteousness of God lives in us forever! Sin's power has been destroyed and the believer is now free to live for God.

> *For sin shall not be your master, because you are not under law, but under grace.*
>
> ### Romans 6:14

---

[103] God did not give us a spirit of timidity, but a spirit of power, of love and of self-discipline. *2 Timothy 1:7*

[104] But the fruit of the Spirit is love, joy, peace, patience, kindness, goodness, faithfulness, gentleness and self-control. *Galatians 5:22*

[105] For the grace of God that brings salvation has appeared to all men. It teaches us to say 'no' to ungodliness and worldly passions, and to live self-controlled, upright and godly lives in this present age, while we wait for the blessed hope – the glorious appearing of our great God and Saviour, Jesus Christ. *Titus 2:11-13*

Neither should we resist or even reject the wonderful message of God's abundant grace. It is a terrible tragedy when a Christian hears the message of his grace and rejects it by saying it is a 'cheap grace' message. I can assure you there is nothing cheap about it; it cost the Son of the living God his life to establish it!

As Christians we need to embrace God's grace, not be cautious of it. We need to embrace it, rejoice in it and allow God to pour it out abundantly over our lives. We are filled with more grace and peace through seeing more of Jesus and his finished work. The more grace you have, the more freedom you will experience and the more power you will have to do exactly what both you and God desire—*that is to walk in the way of love!*

24   Your understanding Father

Praise be to the God and Father of our Lord Jesus Christ, the Father of compassion and the God of all comfort, who comforts us in all our troubles.

2 Corinthians 1:3-4

Sometimes, even as Christians, we face really hard seasons in our life. Sometimes it feels like nobody could possibly understand what we are going through and what we may be suffering with. Even in times when it feels like fellow brothers and sisters in Christ might not be able to understand, we always need to remember that God understands us.

Man sees the outside of a person, but God knows our hearts. God knows our struggles and our pain. When you belong to Christ and believe upon him, God is committed to being your constant help in your times of need.

There are times when you may try to explain yourself to others but they can't understand you or the reasons for certain situations that you have found yourself in. When people misunderstand you, always remember Christ doesn't; he always understands.

You can always come before God and receive comfort. He loves you. He knows you; your weaknesses don't scare God away. He sees the burden you are wrestling with and he wants to empower you to be free from it. He is willing to sit and cry with you. He is willing to walk slowly with you; he cares deeply for you. Look to Jesus, and to what he accomplished on the cross for you, and let him be your strength.

God loves us perfectly, not because of our performance, but because we belong to the one who is perfect in his performance. Because of what Christ has accomplished, we can have assurance that God is forever with us, he forever understands us and he is forever committed to us as his beloved children.

> *Because God has said, 'Never will I leave you; never will I forsake you.' So we say with confidence, 'The Lord is my helper; I will not be afraid. What can man do to me?'*
>
> ### *Hebrews 13:5-6*

Even when we are in the lowest point of our lives, we need to remember to fix our eyes once more upon the beauty of our Saviour. We need to remember that he is still with us because he has promised us that he will never leave us nor forsake us.

Lift up your eyes and place them once again upon Jesus and allow God to transform your life. He sees you as perfect—even now, even in the pit, even in your weakness and humanity, even with your burden, because you believe upon the perfect finished work of your redeemer. Look to Jesus and allow God to freely give you his grace and love in your time of need.[106]

Knowing that it is Jesus who justifies us releases us from always trying to hide ourselves and the situations we find ourselves

---

[106]   Let us then approach the throne of grace with confidence, so that we may receive mercy and find grace to help us in our time of need. *Hebrews 4:16*

in from God. It is the fear of condemnation that pushes us further away from God. We feel fear of condemnation because of the sin and weakness in our Christian lives. Yet it was fear and condemnation that Christ came to destroy in the Christian life! He loves us perfectly; he proved his perfect love for us by dying upon the cross.

He cares for you so much that he embraces you each day to help you in your weakness and times of need. Christ loves you perfectly; this love will never fail you. It is his perfect love that drives out all fear. You can rest in assurance that by the blood of Christ and his perfect finished work of the cross, you can also be free of condemnation.[107]

The simple gospel truth is that you have been made perfect in God's love through your faith in Jesus, and you can live a life without fear, for God is with you and God loves you forever. As a follower of Christ you need to understand that by the work of Christ you are now completely justified in him. When you believe this, you truly begin to live in freedom. You can come before God with freedom and confidence in your weakness to ask *'Lord, I am in need of your grace and mercy, help me in my time of need.'*

When we know we are always justified, even when we are caught in sin and struggles, we can always stand in the presence of God and know that he will help us. It is only by receiving God's grace that we can overcome sin in the first place. In theory, it seems so easy not to sin, but in reality we will always be mastered by sin if we try to overcome it in our own efforts.

Allow yourself to live in God's grace

---

[107]   There is no fear in love. But perfect love drives out fear, because fear has to do with punishment. The one who fears is not made perfect in love. *1 John 4:18*

Allow yourself to live under Gods grace; it is the good news for your life as a believer. God does not want you trapped in sin; he wants you trapped in his love! Allow yourself to live in God's grace and watch God set you free from all of the things that you may have spent years trying to overcome in your own efforts.[108]

---

[108] Because through Christ Jesus the law of the Spirit of life set me free from the law of sin and death. *Romans 8:2*

25   The bride

As a bridegroom rejoices over his bride, so will your God rejoice over
you.

Isaiah 62:5

Let's use our imaginations for a moment. Imagine a single
woman who has no money, no social status and no prospects to
really change her situation in life. To this woman, life seems rather
depressing, quite cruel and unfair. Her situation seems to be pretty
hopeless.

Now imagine one day she meets a man as she is walking
through the city. This man invites her for a coffee and she accepts;
they talk and laugh and have a great time. Imagine the man then
invites her for dinner and she accepts. Now imagine over time this
man falls in love with this woman and asks her to marry him. This
woman can hardly believe the turn of events in her life. Suddenly,
she now has a man in her life, a great man; a man who loves her and
a man who wants to marry her.

Now imagine this was not just your average man, but he was in
fact a multi-billionaire business man. Imagine he has been on the

front cover of TIME magazine. Imagine he literally has everything you could imagine in this world: fame, fortune and great success.

Now, by this stage in our imaginary story we can't help but stop to ask ourselves this one question: why would a man who has everything ask a woman who has nothing to marry him? It seems crazy!

It may seem crazy or highly unlikely, but if it does happen that he falls in love with this woman, does he need a reason for falling in love with her? Does the woman need to be as successful as he is before he can rightly marry her? Does the woman need to have as much wealth as he has before he has the right to fall in love with her? Does she need to earn his marriage proposal?

The truth is that a man doesn't choose to marry a woman because of what she owns. A man chooses a woman to be his bride because he has fallen in love with her and wants to spend the rest of his life with her. Now this woman we have been talking about has been very fortunate indeed. Not only has she become the bride of a man who truly loves her with all of his heart, but she has also now married into all of the benefits and blessings that belong to this man.

Before they were married she had nothing, but now she has everything. Everything that this man owns now also belongs to this woman. She was poor before she married this man, but now she is rich. She was depressed before she married this man but now she is joyful. She had nothing to offer this man except her heart and hand in marriage, and this was all that the man expected from her.

Did she work for all of these blessings she now has? Did she earn all of the good things she now has? No, she didn't. She married into all of these blessings, and praise God that he too has given us a similar experience but so much more glorious!

The Bible refers to the church as the bride of Christ.[109] It really is a profound thought that we are the bride of Christ. We, who had nothing, have met the one who has everything. We who were lonely and depressed have become a joyful community with Christ. Why did Jesus love us so much that he asked us to be united with him for eternity?

The answer surpasses knowledge; it's beyond our human comprehension. It is a glorious reality, one that we can never fully rationalize, but we can praise God that it is the truth! We all share a common history. We had nothing to give Christ except our hearts in devotion to him, and to our amazement that was all he was asking for.

> **The truth is that his love is not something you need to earn**

We have now become the bride of Christ. We were like the woman who had nothing and no hope, and by God's grace we have been united in Spirit with the one who has everything. We had nothing to give, but Jesus was not looking for anything to receive, for he already had everything. He was not looking for gifts, he was looking for a bride he could pour out his unfailing love upon, and that bride is the church. You, united with everyone who calls on the name of Jesus, are that bride!

Before we were saved by Christ, we really had nothing to offer God. Despite our lack, Jesus loved us and he invited us to become part of his church, his bride. This kind of love truly surpasses understanding, his love is unfailing and glorious and by the grace of God it is poured out upon us all.

---

[109] For this reason a man will leave his father and mother and be united to his wife, and the two will become one flesh." This is a profound mystery—but I am talking about Christ and the church. *Ephesians 5:31-32*

(God) who has called us to a holy life—not by anything we have done but by his own purpose and grace.

2 Timothy 1:9

Christ does not love us in this way based on our lives, it is based on his own life! If we try to figure out why Jesus loves us based on our efforts and spiritual devotion, we will fail miserably to ever find an answer.

The reason he loves us so much, that he washes away our sins and makes us co-heirs of heaven with him, is based solely on his life. The giving of his love is not a response to our actions; it is the DNA of his nature. It is because Jesus is love. It is who he is, and so it is what he gives to us! We will never be able to accept such radical love if we keep trying to understand it through our old religious mind-sets.

The truth is that his love is not something you need to earn. It is something you need to receive. When you can receive it as a gift from God, then you can receive it in abundance.

The truth is that you are loved, not according to your performance but according to God's own purpose and grace. Look at your Lord and Saviour in all his glory, in all his grace, in all his love and thank God that Christ loves you apart from your performance. He doesn't love you because you have somehow proved that he should love you by your good works, he loves you simply because you said 'yes' and became part of his bride.

You said 'yes' to his invitation of salvation and relationship. Because of this you have become one with Jesus and are no longer bound to condemnation. You are now bound in his unfailing love forever!

26 Our salvation

Do not be afraid, little flock, for your Father has been pleased to give you the kingdom!

Luke 12:32

It really is beyond imagination. That the Almighty creator of the heavens, who designed the entire universe in all of it's majesty as well as the earth in all of it's detail, would offer us a better best friend, a better leader and a better hope than ourselves. He has given us his very own Son.

All of us share a similar moment in time. It was the moment we heard the good news of Jesus, and having believed, we were included in Christ. In this moment we went from being distant from God to being even more than a friend, we became children of God![110]

We didn't earn our salvation, but Christ earned it for us. We didn't deserve to be favoured because of our own works and effort,

---

[110]   And you also were included in Christ when you heard the word of truth, the gospel of your salvation. Having believed, you were marked in him with a seal, the promised Holy Spirit. *Ephesians 1:13*

but we were included in Christ who has earned God's full favour on our behalf through his perfect atoning sacrifice upon the cross. As Christians, we do not boast in our own goodness, we boast in the goodness of Christ. Our boast is not that we have earned our holiness, righteousness and redemption. Our boast is in Christ, who has become for us, our holiness, righteousness and redemption.

Everything that we have is a gift from God based on our belief upon Jesus. It's amazing to know that even our holiness is a gift. We are not just holy, but we have actually become *the* holiness of Christ. That means that when God wants to define his holiness he simply points to you! If you are in Christ then you have become his holiness, his righteousness and his redemption.

This blessedness is not only for the moment we are included in Christ, but for every day we walk on earth and for eternity to come. You are forever in the position of blessing. You are forever loved. You are forever forgiven. You are forever favoured. You are forever accepted. You are forever credited as righteous, holy and blameless in God's sight. You are forever set free. Not by your efforts, but because you belong to Christ. This is the good news for your life!

> We can't ear
> anything fro
> God for the ve
> fact that Chris
> has earned it a
> for us alread

For many believers, when we first believed in Christ we were so in awe of his greatness. As time went on we began to take our eyes off of Jesus and place them back onto ourselves. This is a common process that has a domino effect which leads a believer back into a false religious mindset, instead of remaining in our glorious new covenant reality. When we do this, we become self-focused (or ministry-focused, or church program-focused) and not Christ-focused. The result of changing our focus is a change in our relationship with God.

Instead of thanking God that we are included in Jesus, our prayers become consumed with how sorry we are to God. Not sorry that we have sinned, but sorry that we are just not better Christians. We work harder for God, but feel less worthy of his presence. We begin to believe that we have to do everything for God (work harder in our ministry, work harder to build the church programs, work harder in our prayer life!)

When we begin to believe that we have to earn everything from God we start living by worldly principles instead of by the reality of Christ. Instead of remaining in the truth that we receive all things from God because we belong to Christ, we begin to believe some other fine sounding argument that doesn't depend on the reality of Christ at all. It is this very problem that the Apostle Paul addresses with the Colossian church.

> *See to it that no one takes you captive through hollow and deceptive philosophy, which depends on human tradition and the basic principles of this world rather than on Christ.*

> **Colossians 2:8**

We can't earn anything from God for the very fact that Christ has earned it all for us already. Christ now gives everything to us as a gift from God. As Christians we need to remind ourselves why God sees us the way that he does and why God favours us the way that he does. It is based on Christ's finished work, not our unfinished work.

The simple gospel truth is that we have not earned any of the blessing and benefits of God, but we have freely received them from God because we belong to his Son, Jesus Christ. We, as the church, need to take our eyes off of ourselves and place them once again upon Jesus and his perfect life and sacrifice. When we do this, suddenly everything starts to make sense; we begin to accept that we really are loved, accepted, holy, righteous, blameless and favoured.

We don't accept this reality based on our works, but based on God's abundant provision of grace![111]

All of these blessings belong to Christ, all of the promises belong to Christ, the fullness of the Holy Spirit belongs to Christ, and the kingdom of God belongs to Christ. It all belongs completely to Christ. No one else could ever earn, buy or deserve them. By the grace of God when you believed in Christ you were placed in him and you were credited with all of this.

The good news of Jesus Christ is that in him and through him we can rejoice that God has now given to us his kingdom of peace, righteousness and joy in the Holy Spirit.

---

[111]   From the fullness of his grace we have all received one blessing after another. *John 1:16*

27   The church

Finally, my brothers, rejoice in the Lord! It is no trouble for me to write the same things to you again, and it is a safeguard for you.

Philippians 3:1

As the church, when we come around the grace of God and together behold the glory of who Jesus is, rejoice in his goodness and share around his beauty, something amazing happens. We are supernaturally set free of our burdens, and we are filled with an inexpressible joy. The church can never be free if our focus is on something else, even if it is a seemingly godly and good thing to focus on. Our focus needs to remain on the grace of God that is found in Jesus Christ.

If we focus our teaching on being morally good people over preaching about the greatness of Jesus, then we will not be free or fruitful. If we focus on evangelism, serving people or building the programs in our churches over focusing on the greatness of Jesus, then we will not be free or fruitful. However, if we focus on the greatness of Jesus we can not help but be free, be full of faith, be united and be overflowing with joy!

When we take our eyes off of ourselves and place them together upon Jesus, the Spirit of the Lord rejoices, and where the Spirit of the Lord is, there is freedom. More than this, when our focus remains together on the greatness of Jesus, then all other areas also actually become fruitful.

When his finished work remains our focus, the whole church is transformed by the Spirit and bears much good fruit in our lives.

When the finished work of Jesus remains our focus, the other areas of the Christian life also become much more fruitful than they ever could be when they become our priority over Christ.

When we focus on the perfect love of Jesus, evangelism happens and is fruitful because the Spirit does the work through us. When we focus on the power of Jesus to establish our new covenant of grace, serving people happens and is fruitful because the Spirit does the work through us. When we focus on the greatness of Jesus, the church is built according to God's divine plan because the Spirit adds new believers to it daily.

The church is the body of Christ. It is the community of believers who believe upon Jesus as their Lord and Saviour. Jesus promised to build this community. He doesn't expect us to do it for him because he knows that we can't do it! The church is not a physical building; it is not like the temple of the Old Testament. The church is a spiritual reality that is built by Christ as he adds more people into himself through faith.[112]

We can embrace new believers into God's family, but we can't make them a new creation, that work is done solely by the Holy Spirit. It is by the Spirit of Christ that people are added to the

---

[112]   In him the whole building is joined together and rises to become a holy temple in the Lord. And in him you too are being built together to become a dwelling in which God lives by his Spirit. *Ephesians 2:21-22*

church, not by our will-power and efforts. It is our job to do the beholding, and God's job to do the adding.[113]

I am not saying that as Christians we should purposely do nothing. Remember beholding Jesus is not about staring at a picture of him hanging on a wall. What I am saying is that we need to recognise that it is not ourselves that do good works; it is the grace of God in us that does them. It is always God's Spirit that does the doing. As Paul the Apostle explained with regards to his own ministry.

> *But by the grace of God I am what I am, and his grace to me was not without effect. No, I worked harder than all of them—yet not I, but the grace of God that was with me.*
>
> ### *1 Corinthians 15:10*

Paul acknowledged that God had used his life to do many things, but it was not Paul who did them, it was the grace of God within him. This is the attitude we all need to have, without it we become proud too easily and end up boasting in our own good works that we are doing for God. We fail to see that it was not ourselves at all, but Christ in us who was doing the good works in the first place.

When we rest in Christ we can allow our attention to be upon his perfect finished work that was done on our behalf. When this is our focus we rest in assurance in him instead of being restless due to a fear of failure and a fear of not doing enough for God.

The spirit of the world works in restless people, but the Spirit of Christ works in rested Christians! When we rest in Christ with

---

[113] Every day they continued to meet together in the temple courts. They broke bread in their homes and ate together with glad and sincere hearts, praising God and enjoying the favour of all the people. And the Lord added to their number daily those who were being saved. *Acts 2:46-47*

complete assurance, it gives the Spirit access to do many good works through our lives.

For some it may result in the Spirit working through them in the area of sharing their faith and testimony. For others it may result in the Spirit working through them in the area of service to the poor, to the community or to their families. To others still it may result in the Spirit working through them to help lead and administrate different aspects of the church community.[114]

> **The spirit of the world works in restless people, but the Spirit of Christ works in rested Christians!**

There are many different ways that the Spirit works in and through us, too many to list of course. We are all part of the body of Christ and we all have a different role to play. Each of us have been given gifts, and as we behold Christ, the Spirit directs each of us individually on how and where he wants us to outwork those gifts to the glory of God.

As the church, we *lose no time* or productivity by spending *all of our time* seeking to see more of Jesus. Likewise, a preacher gives the church the most practical message possible when he speaks of nothing but the greatness of Christ. The preacher does not need to tell the church how to live good and productive lives, he needs to uphold *the Life* himself! The preacher needs to let the church behold the way, the truth and the life and be transformed by believing upon him!

Some people might disagree and say, 'how will we know how to live good and moral lives if we are not taught it and shown the way?' The answer is that we will know the way because 'the way' is

[114] Now you are the body of Christ, and each one of you is a part of it. *1 Corinthians 12:27*

living and active in us. The Holy Spirit of Jesus is living in us, and Jesus promised that his Spirit will guide us into all truth.[115]

As Christians, we don't need to continually hear laws, life application principles or moral teaching to know the way to live; we need to hear more about Jesus. We need to hear more about his person so that we can trust more in his perfect finished work accomplished for us and his loving guidance now actively at work in us.

The more preachers proclaim the greatness of Jesus, the greater fruit the believers will produce. The Apostle Peter reminds us in his second letter that it is not by gaining more knowledge on how to live that we are transformed, but by gaining more knowledge of Jesus Christ! The more you know about the greatness of Christ, the more God pours out his grace upon your life in abundance. The more grace you receive, the more fruit God can produce in and through your life, to the glory of God.

> *Grace and peace be yours in abundance through the knowledge of God and of Jesus our Lord.*
>
> **2 Peter 1:2**

When we are continually conscious of whom Christ is in our lives and rest in the assurance that comes from belonging to him, God multiplies the productivity and fruitfulness of our lives. This is what separates the Christian faith from every other religion. Where other religions expect the believer to do *good works for* their god, the Christian is expected to rest in *the goodness of* God! When we do this as followers of Christ, it allows God to pour his grace into our lives and do many good works through us.

---

[115]   I have much more to say to you, more than you can now bear. But when he, the Spirit of truth, comes, he will guide you into all truth. *John 16:12-13*

The Apostle Paul lived his whole life this way. No matter how many good works he did for the Lord he never wanted to talk about them, in fact he called his good works rubbish in comparison to the greatness of knowing Christ. He only wanted to tell the early church more about Jesus.[116] When we focus on simply knowing Christ, the Spirit accomplishes an abundance of good works through our lives, but we never find our boast in them.

---

[116] What is more, I consider everything a loss compared to the surpassing greatness of knowing Christ Jesus my Lord, for whose sake I have lost all things. I consider them rubbish, that I may gain Christ and be found in him, not having a righteousness of my own that comes from the law, but that which is through faith in Christ—the righteousness that comes from God and is by faith. *Philippians 3:8-9*

28   The preacher

Although I am less than the least of all God's people, this grace was given me: to preach to the Gentiles the unsearchable riches of Christ.

Ephesians 3:8

Preachers and teachers are gifts to the body of Christ. They are given to us to build us up in our wonderful faith. They have been given grace by the Lord for a particular task, and that task is to lift up the greatness, the glory and the beauty of Jesus Christ.

It is the role of the preacher to exalt Jesus and proclaim the boundless riches of Christ, to uphold Jesus and to boast in him. It is not the role of the preacher to simply preach about biblical thoughts and ideas, but to preach about Jesus! Not to preach only about what we should do to be like Jesus, but whom he is!

The four gospels give us a great account of the miracles that Jesus performed when he walked on earth. These miracles are all a testimony to the greatness of Jesus. Yet when you read the letters Paul, Peter and John wrote to the early church you will find that they never discuss any of the miracles Jesus did in their letters.

They never talk about any of his miracles on earth except for his perfect finished work of the cross.

Of course they believed that all of his miracles happened, Peter and John were actually eyewitnesses to them all. However, their hearts were motivated not to preach about things Jesus did, but to preach about who he is! The miracles he did were amazing, but the Apostles seemed more amazed at whom he is rather than what miracles he performed!

God calls the preacher to *uphold* Jesus, so that the church can *behold* Jesus. It is the purpose of the church to rejoice in the proclamation of the boundless riches of Christ and to thank God that we can boast in him all of the days of our lives with joy and gladness. When a preacher fails to understand this, the result is a terrible mixed message that ultimately causes those who sit under their message to be more conscious of the sin of men then they are of the righteousness of God.

Even today there are many preachers instructing Christians to believe the Holy Spirit is in their lives to convict them that they are sinning. This may sound religiously right to many, but it is simply not in line with the truth of the gospel. I am not saying God is not concerned about sin, but you must understand that as a disciple it is not the ministry of the Holy Spirit to point out sin in your life. The Holy Spirit's ministry is to point out your righteousness. That righteousness is not an action, it is a person who is living in you, his name is Jesus and he is your hope of glory!

The Scriptures do not tell us that the Holy Spirit is pointing out sins in a believer. There may be parts of Scripture where the Holy Spirit is pointing out sins to unbelievers, but not to those who are in Christ. When we read the Bible we find that the Holy Spirit is pointing out to all of us who are in Christ our right-standing in Christ. The Holy Spirit is reminding us of the righteousness of

Christ in us, because he understands more than anyone that this revelation is the power of God in our life.

So where does this 'sin-conscious' teaching originate from? It mainly comes from pastors and preachers misinterpreting the words of Jesus in the gospel of John.

When the Holy Spirit comes he will convict the world of sin, right-eousness and judgement.

John 16:8

It is this Scripture that many well-meaning preachers point to as their foundational text in order to prove their belief that the Holy Spirit is convicting the believer of sin. I'm sure Jesus must have known how quickly preachers would take these words out of context, so much so that he actually interprets for us the true meaning in the very next verse.

In regard to sin, because men do not believe in me.

John 16:9

Jesus tells us that the sin that the Holy Spirit will convict people of is the sin of unbelief.

> God calls the preacher to uphold Jesus, so that the church can behold Jesus

Do you believe upon Jesus? If not, then even now the Holy Spirit can convict your heart of your unbelief, so that you may turn to Jesus and accept him for who he truly is. You can be assured that he loves you, that he died for you and that he wants you to live eternally with him. The good news for your life is that forgiveness, new life and eternal salvation is available for you today![117]

---

[117] But what does it say? 'The word is near you; it is in your mouth and in your heart,' that is, the word of faith we are proclaiming: That if you confess with your mouth, 'Jesus is Lord,' and believe in your heart that God raised him from the dead, you will be saved. For it is

If you have already accepted Jesus, then the Holy Spirit is no longer trying to convict you of sin, he is now trying to convince you of your righteousness in Christ. He is testifying that you are loved. He is testifying that because Christ became sin upon the cross, you have now become the righteousness of God. He is testifying that you are forever accepted by God, and that he has forever forgiven and forever forgotten all of your sins. He is testifying to you that what he now remembers everyday is your belief upon his Son!

The truth is that the Holy Spirit is continually looking at the greatness of Christ and testifying to us that we belong to him. All of us as disciples need to die to our self-focus and live with a Christ-focus. We are a new creation in Christ; we have been created with a new nature. Not a sinful nature, but a righteous nature. When we start believing who we are in Christ, then we will start seeing the results the Bible promises us. More than that, we also finally begin to understand Jesus and know him better![118]

As Christians, we need to take our eyes off of ourselves. We need to resist the temptation to focus on our failings. We also need to resist the temptation to boast in our ministries and our successes. Our boast needs to be upon Christ and his perfect finished work. It is only this focus that fills us with joy, peace, security, and grace![119]

---

with your heart that you believe and are justified, and it is with your mouth that you confess and are saved. *Romans 10:8-10*

[118] I keep asking that the God of our Lord Jesus Christ, the glorious Father, may give you the Spirit of wisdom and revelation, so that you may know him better. *Ephesians 1:17*

[119] Praise be to the God and Father of our Lord Jesus Christ, who has blessed us in the heavenly realms with every spiritual blessing in Christ. *Ephesians 1:3*

29 The Corinthians

Do you not know that your body is a temple of the Holy Spirit, who is in you, whom you have received from God?

1 Corinthians 6:19

When we look at the Corinthian church we see that many members were weak and involved in sin. They were doing all sorts of things that were not in step with the Spirit. Yet the Apostle Paul's way of bringing the Christians out of living in sin was not to smack them over the head with the law, but to remind them of who they were in Christ.

He never wanted any members of the church to fall captive to sin, and Paul was never one to ignore the problem. However, he knew that making them focus on themselves and their weaknesses would only make them weaker and ultimately more susceptible to sin.

He pointed them back to the greatness of Christ; that through the perfect finished work of the cross they had all been made new creations in Christ. He continually reminded the church of the gift of righteousness that had been given to them. He did this because he knew the reason sin was in the church in the first place was because the church was self-focused, having taken their eyes off of the gift-giver and having focused instead on the gifts.

Paul knew the way for the church to die to sin and walk in step with the Spirit was to fix their eyes back onto Christ and understand that they had been made into new creations, that they were the temple of the Holy Spirit. When we keep our eyes on the greatness of Christ and live by his grace alone it causes us to walk in the truth of our identity in Christ, in step with the Spirit and free from sin.[120]

When God made us into new creations it was permanent. This is how God now sees us. Even when we stumble, even when we fail, even when we find ourselves in weakness, we can stand before God with freedom and confidence and say, 'thank you Lord that you have made me a new creation in Christ and that is how you now see me.' When we have this confidence, we don't hide from God when we are weak and failing in our faith journey, we come before him with confidence and receive his mercy and grace in our time of need.[121]

Paul teaches us all the profound Christian virtue of looking at each other within the church through the eyes of Christ and seeing the new creation, not the old.

Choose to see Jesus in your fellow brothers and sisters in the church, the body of Christ. We need to build each other up in the faith by pointing out our righteousness in Christ. We need to speak about who we are in Christ with each other, and speak about his greatness and his new covenant of grace with his church. When we

---

[120] Since we live by the Spirit, let us keep in step with the Spirit. *Galatians 5:25*

[121] Let us then approach the throne of grace with confidence, so that we may receive mercy and find grace to help us in our time of need. *Hebrews 4:16*

consistently do this, we find ourselves supernaturally overflowing with the fruit of love and the bond of peace.

30 The Galatians

I am astonished that you are so quickly deserting the one who called you by the grace of Christ and are turning to a different gospel—which is really no gospel at all. Evidently some people are throwing you into confusion and are trying to pervert the gospel of Christ.

Galatians 1:6-7

When we read Paul's letter to the Galatians we read about a very serious problem. The problem was not that the Galatians were indulging in sexual immorality or some other obvious sin. There was not an outbreak of obvious immoral behaviour. So what was the problem? The problem was that the Galatians wanted to start earning the favour of God by their own efforts.

Paul wrote to the Galatians that this is not just some slight difference in doctrine, but that they were turning to a belief that is a completely different gospel! He went on to say that it is in fact no gospel at all. For there is only one gospel, and that is the gospel of God's grace. Believing that we need to earn God's favour is not the gospel at all, but a lie that destroys the faith of a believer and causes them to fall away from God's abundant provision of grace.

You who are trying to be justified by law have been alienated from Christ; you have fallen away from grace.

Galatians 5:4

The Galatians church started off their journey of faith believing in Paul's gospel message of the greatness of Christ and his finished work. They believed the message that Jesus fulfilled the old covenant through his perfect life, bringing it to an end, and then established by his perfect finished work upon the cross a new covenant for all nations.

When they believed this the whole church was free and full of joy. Their boast was not in themselves but in the greatness of Christ. However, over time they changed their beliefs. They were deceived by false teachers who were preaching a mixed gospel message of law and grace; old and new. The result was a confused church that began to want to please God by their efforts and good works.

They started to believe that this was the foundation on which God would see them as righteous. Basically, they started getting religious! No longer did they believe that they had received the gift of righteousness, now they believed that by their efforts and their 'holy obligations' they were righteous. They no longer believed that they were blessed because they belonged to Christ, but because they were being obedient to the law! Paul was perplexed. How could this have happened? He wrote to them and asked:

You foolish Galatians! Who has bewitched you? Before your very eyes Jesus Christ was clearly portrayed as crucified. I would like to learn just one thing from you: Did you receive the Spirit by observing the law, or by believing what you heard? Are you so foolish? After beginning with the Spirit, are you now trying to attain your goal by human effort? Have you suffered so much for nothing—if it really was for nothing? Does God give you his Spirit and work mira-

*cles among you because you observed the law, or because you be-
lieved what you heard?*

Galatians 3:1-5

Paul was trying to get the Galatians to come back to the simple
truth of the good news of Jesus Christ: it is not our efforts of godliness that place us in right-standing with God—*it is because we believe what we have heard!* It is because we believe upon the perfect
finished work of Christ and receive the gift of his grace and righteousness.

As Christians, we all start out completely in God's grace, saved
by the perfect finished work of Christ. Over time however we can
easily fall into the same trap as the Galatians. We can begin to believe upon our own works instead of Christ's perfect finished work.
We can begin to focus on our godliness instead of the perfect God
who died for us. We can begin to fix our eyes on our efforts instead
of fixing our eyes on the greatness of Christ.

The Galatians needed to place their eyes back upon Jesus and
remember what he had accomplished on their behalf; we too are
greatly blessed when we do this. We can joyfully give Christ the
credit he deserves and, at the same time, allow the Spirit to work in
and through us by his strength.

Jesus is more than enough for our salvation. We have the honour of looking at his greatness and believing in the truth of what we
have heard—that is the good news of the perfect finished work of
Christ. We accept the grace, that has been given through him, and
the Spirit transforms us to shine his glory through our lives and
into the world.

When God looks at you he sees you neither in your weaknesses
nor your good works. The truth is that he sees you in Christ. That is
his focus, and that is why he considers you perfect, holy and righteous—*because God sees you in Christ*. He sees your faith upon Christ

and his perfect finished work on the cross. He sees your thankfulness that Christ has paid for all of your forgiveness and all of your blessings. He looks at you and sees you in Christ; allow yourself to see the Christ in you as well. You are a new creation in him, and he is your true reality.[122]

---

[122]   And my God will meet all your needs according to his glorious riches in Christ Jesus. *Philippians 4:19*

Conclusion: You are radically loved

But we ought always to thank God for you, brothers loved by the Lord, because from the beginning God chose you to be saved through the sanctifying work of the Spirit and through belief in the truth. He called you to this through our gospel, that you might share in the glory of our Lord Jesus Christ.

2 Thessalonians 2:13-14

Why is it so important to see the finished work of Jesus? It's important because when we see all that he has done for us it allows us to truly rest in the radical love of God. It is in this place of resting in his love for us that the Spirit supernaturally shines that revelation into our relationships and into the world around us.

When you rest in the truth of how much Christ loves you, you find yourself starting to love others with the same kind of love. When you understand how much patience Christ has for you, you begin to have the same kind of patience for others. When you understand how much grace God gives to you, you begin to have the same kind of grace for others.

What is the greatest blessing we as Christians can receive? It is the blessing of knowing Christ and being found in him. He is so wonderful, just belonging to him is more than enough to live a peaceful and joyful life. God has so many gifts and so many blessings that he wants to give us as believers in Christ, but as great as they all are, they are incomparable with the blessing of simply knowing Christ Jesus as our Lord.

We can rest in Jesus and have hearts that proclaim: 'Lord, you are enough for me!' When God sees this to be the confession of our hearts it makes him smile, and I'm sure he says to us, 'that really is wonderful, but I'm still going to give you all the rest of my blessings as well!'

The more we look to Jesus and believe in our hearts that he is more than enough for us, the more love increases in our hearts, we receive more peace and we overflow with more joy. When we see Jesus for who he truly is and declare, 'Lord, my eyes are fixed on you, you are more than enough for me!' the Spirit gets so excited that he can't wait to fill us with the fullness of all of the likeness of Christ!

We, the community of God's people, who believe in the perfect finished work of Christ, are the church. We each individually have the privilege of beholding Jesus and seeing him for who he truly is, the perfect one who through his perfect sacrifice has made us perfect forever in the eyes of God!

Look to him for who he is and by the Spirit of God be transformed. Each new day, as we look to Christ, we will discover more of the treasures, the glory, the power, the beauty and the majesty of Christ. We will also find ourselves coming together with thankful and joyful hearts, knowing the truth of his love for us with an ever increasing understanding.

My purpose is that they may be encouraged in heart and united in love, so that they may have the full riches of complete understanding, in order that they may know the mystery of God, namely, Christ, in whom are hidden all the treasures of wisdom and knowledge.

Colossians 2:2-3

You are a new creation. You are the holiness and righteousness of God. You are without blemish in God's eyes. You are his beloved child. You are perfectly united with him. All of this has been accomplished by the grace and power and perfect atoning sacrifice of Christ, to whom you now belong. You are so loved and are now standing in the very place where God's abundant provision of grace flows in your life. You are 'in' the Son of the living God!

Therefore, since we have been justified through faith we have peace with God through our Lord Jesus Christ, through whom we have gained access by faith into this grace in which we now stand, and we rejoice in the hope of the glory of God.

Romans 5:1-2

Rejoice! You are living in a covenant relationship with the almighty God based on his divine faithfulness, his perfect finished work and his unfailing love!

This is the reality of Jesus: *He is everything, and you are everything to him.* You are his treasured possession. You are his love.

The simple gospel truth is actually the most profound truth anyone could ever know. You know it and you believe it. Now enjoy it.

You are radically loved.

Acknowledgments

This book was a long journey from start to finish, and I'm thankful that I had some cheerful companions who offered me their support, as well as their various professional skills, along the way. I would like to take the opportunity to express my gratitude to those who so generously helped bring my book to completion.

I would like to thank Yannick Ulich, Art Henkel and Daniel Bretschneider for their proof-reading and editorial assistance, with a special thank-you specifically to Veronica Hall, who generously offered to be the final editor; your input and expertise made such a big difference.

I would also like to thank Annabel Schubert for designing the cover art. I appreciate how you so graciously put up with all the changes I kept suggesting along the way.

Finally, I would like to thank my family, especially my wife Mira, who supported and encouraged me throughout the whole process, and also my Mum, who has always been an inspiring role model as well as my biggest fan. Thank you for always believing in me, and instilling in me the confidence to always pursue the dreams God has placed in my heart.

And of course, I have to thank Jesus, who not only finished the work of salvation for us all, but also worked his grace in me to finish this book. Thanks for, well, everything!

About the author

Mick Mooney is a passionate communicator of God's grace. He is a preacher, author and also the creator of the popular 'Searching for Grace' comic strip (www.searchingforgrace.com). He is originally from Australia and currently resides in Germany with his wife Mira.

Manufactured by Amazon.ca
Bolton, ON